Paris by Pastry: Stalking the Sweet
Life on the Streets of Paris

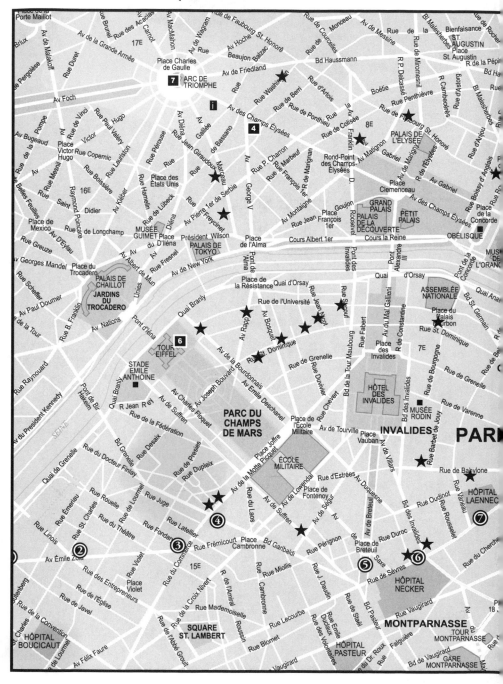

Map of Paris

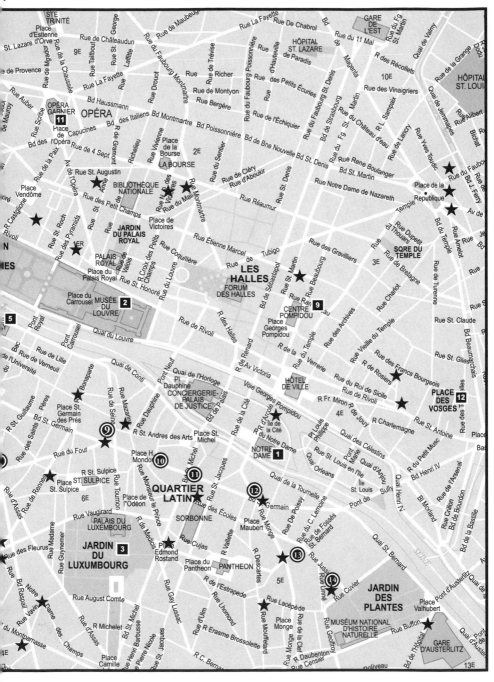

★ Pâtisseries

▪ Attractions

◉ Seine à Seine Metro Stops

Paris by Pastry
Stalking the Sweet Life on the Streets of Paris

JOYCE SLAYTON MITCHELL

JONES
BOOKS
Madison, Wisconsin

Jones Books
309 N. Hillside Ter.
Madison, Wisconsin 53705-3328
www.jonesbooks.com

First printing, first edition

Book and cover design by Janet Trembley

Photographs by Joyce Slayton Mitchell

Library of Congress Cataloging-in-Publication Data

Mitchell, Joyce Slayton.
  Paris by pastry : stalking the sweet life on the streets of paris / by Joyce Slayton
Mitchell.
      p. cm.
  Includes bibliographical references and index.
  ISBN 0-9763539-6-2 (alk. paper)
  1. Pastry—France—Paris. 2. Cookery, French. I. Title.
  TX773.M547 2006
  641.8'650944361—dc22
                                        2006004144

Printed in the U.S.A.

Contents

Table of Contents

Preface

People are different. Some like to visit a foreign city and first see everything on the "top attractions" list—that is, the most popular sights, what everyone has told them not to miss. Others like to see the top three and then take off exploring on their own. Still, some travelers make a point never to go near the Eiffel Tower in Paris, Piccadilly Circus in London, or St. Peter's in Rome. (Georgette tends to be a little like that. If it's trendy, she doesn't want it.)

Usually what you go to see depends on how much time you have. For example, if you are on a group tour you may have three days in Paris. Or even one day! Or you may be on a tour for five days in Paris with only one afternoon "free." You could be a student and in Paris for the year. Or for a semester, or for summer school. If you are traveling for business, you may have planned your European travel to include one day in Paris on your way to Madrid or Israel. Whatever your time and reason, if you're the kind of traveler who wants to skip the big-time attractions and see special-interest things such as the stock market, a major library, a university, or a museum where the art is up and the crowds are down, you may want to turn directly to the "Paris Prizes: According to Jeanette and Georgette" chapter. If you have the time and you are a methodical person (Jeanette tends to be a little like that), you may want to start at the beginning of the book with "Paris Prizes: Top Attractions," go straight to Notre-Dame, and then do it all! Whatever your personality, whatever your Parisian interest and time, J. *et* G. know that you are in for the greatest travel treat of all: *Paris by Pastry.*

Acknowledgments

I want to start right off by expressing my thankfulness that my primary source for this book is the City of Light itself—Paris. From the first through the twentieth *arrondissements*, this magnificently beautiful city was observed, studied, touched, and tasted, providing the sweetest life in the world.

I owe special thanks to Françoise Maleyran, my Parisian friend in whose home I was always welcomed, and a friend who would check and double-check a phone number, statue, or French pastry recipe on the spur of the moment. *À la tienne, Françoise*!

It is a pleasure to thank Joan Strasbaugh, Publisher, Jones Books, for her excitement and enthusiasm for *Paris by Pastry*. Particular thanks, too, goes to Carrie Bebris, editor *extraordinaire*, who conscientiously edited the English, the French, the fractured-French, the Paris streets, and the Web sites. As the writer of thirty-five books, I know what I am talking about when I say that Jones Books knows what they are doing! *Merci mille fois, mesdames!*

My brother John R. Slayton was brought up with the same high standards of taste for all foods eaten only in season and with the purest of ingredients in our home. He often joined me in Paris to help out with the tasting research. John's support is constant and unsurpassed.

I will be forever grateful to my Paris pastry-hunting pal and co-taster, Beverly A. Thomas, who has played a significant role in the research of this book. Also known as Jeanette throughout the guide, she has my admiration for her depth of knowledge of French history, literature, and language. Jeanette's persistence in getting the details right is unparalleled. At the same time, it is important for my dear readers to understand that any errors that they may find in French grammar all belong to Georgette, not to Jeanette!

Paris by Pastry is dedicated to all of you who soon will be stalking the sweet life on the streets of Paris. Dear reader: Take your time. Choose carefully. Take a bite. Savor it. Swallow before you take the second bite. *Regarde. Goûte. Apprécie—amuse-toi!*

Georgette, a.k.a.
Joyce Slayton Mitchell
Paris, France

Introduction

The best pastries in the world are found in the pâtisserie shops of Paris. It isn't easy for Americans. We are used to sitting down for a cup of coffee and getting whatever we want to go with it. It doesn't seem like asking too much to expect a one-stop pastry and cup of coffee. The French, unlike Americans, do not plan for a pastry, a coffee, and a seat in one place. In Paris, the very best pastries are not in the restaurants and coffee bars. They are found in a beautiful pastry shop—a delicious luxury taken for granted by the French. Every neighborhood, many where Americans have yet to visit, has its own delectable, traditional pâtisserie. Often passed down in the family from generation to generation, the pastry shop has a permanent place in Parisian *quartiers* (neighborhoods); many pâtisseries are easily distinguished by their 19th-century paintings on glass at the entrance or corner of the buildings. Parisians frequent the same pastry shop day in and day out.

Jeanette and Georgette are eager for their fellow Americans to learn that if they want the best in Parisian pastries, they must be bought in the *quartiers* and carried to the Louvre or Champs-Elysées or Montmartre areas where little residential grocery shopping takes place. Like the Parisians, Americans can go to the residential neighborhoods and find the very best in every single *arrondissement* of Paris.

A word about Paris and arrondissements (districts). Arrondissements are important in Paris and every street sign (usually attached one flight up on the buildings at the corner of each street) always includes the arrondissement number. Addresses in Paris are designated by a "750" followed by the arrondissement number. Therefore, if you look up the address of the Tour Eiffel, you will see that it is Champ-de-Mars and the zip code is 75007. Or if you look up hotels and restaurants before you go, you will immediately know where in Paris they are by their 750 zip code and whatever arrondissement in which it is located: 06, 07, perhaps the *très, très, chic* famous 16th. Arrondissements and *quartiers* (neighborhoods) tend to be distinctive. There are twenty arrondissements and *Paris by Pastry* will take you to every single one of them! Before you know it, you will be describing the neighborhoods of Paris to your friends from your own observations of each arrondissement.

Paris by Pastry features pastry shops near tourist attractions, as well as around centers of Parisian life where tourists seldom venture, and even on a "pastry-line" metro. This new and exciting guide to Paris is designed for J. *et* G.'s dear readers to satisfy that eternal sweet-tooth craving . . . to join Jeanette and Georgette's Paris adventures in hunting and capturing the most magnificent pastries in the world!

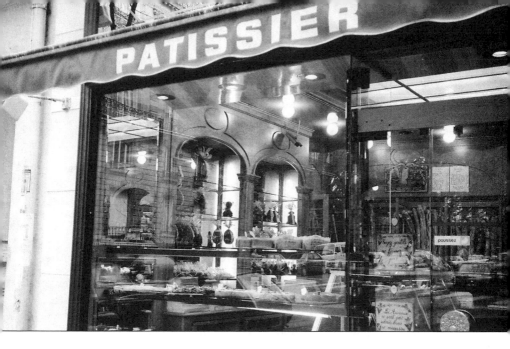

Paris Prizes
Top Attractions

When you tell your friends that you have been to Paris, they will assume that you have seen the top attractions. If you are on a tour, no tour leader would even think of taking you for a day in Paris without seeing the Cathedral of Notre-Dame, the Eiffel Tower, the Louvre, and the Champs-Elysées. If you were there for only a day, maybe you wouldn't get to the Orsay Museum or the Luxembourg Gardens, but when you say you've been to Paris, the expectation is that you know these top attractions. Therefore, if you are the kind of traveler who wants to see what is expected of you, then by all means start right off stalking the sweet streets of Paris with "Paris Prizes: Top Attractions!"

Cathedral of Notre-Dame

Place du Parvis-Notre-Dame, Paris 04
Telephone: 01.43.26.07.39
Metro: Cité
Bus: 21, 38, 47, 85, 96

The Cathedral of Notre-Dame is a thrilling place to begin your *Paris by Pastry* visit because it is *kilomètre zéro* for all of France. Hurry to Notre-Dame by metro, bus, or foot. Stand facing the cathedral, look down, and there you will find in the plaza the *kilomètre zéro* brass circle from where all national highways connecting Paris to other parts of France begin. You'll be hungry because it will still be morning after disembarking an early morning plane, dropping off your luggage, picking up your *carte orange* for €15.40 in the metro station for a week's bus and metro transportation, and finally arriving at the Cathedral of Notre-Dame.

Now. Where to get that first scrumptious pastry? Standing at point zero facing Notre-Dame, you will see the closest pastry shop on your left on rue du Cloître-Notre-Dame, parallel to the length of Notre-Dame. That shop is Aux Tours de Notre-Dame, with a very ordinary selection of *tarte aux pommes* (apple tarts), *tartes du jour*, and *éclairs*. Realizing that you are in Paris for the very best of pastries, you will naturally walk right by this place and the line of souvenir shops with lunch places and food not worth your tasting, where there is no pastry over a "4" (on a scale of 1 to 10). But still on your left, if you walk away from the junk on rue du Cloître-Notre-Dame to 1, rue d'Arcole, the adjacent street leading to the

Seine—*voilà*! There is a gem within a block of "point zero." Like many pastry shops in Paris, the name is a generic

Pâtisserie–Boulangerie Eurl Junior
1, rue d'Arcole, Paris 04
Telephone: 01.43.54.78.49
Metro: Cité
Closed: Sundays pm

With a small showcase of the tops in pastry options around Notre-Dame (nothing below a 7), you will find *mille-feuilles* (napoleons), *tartlettes aux ananas* (pineapple tarts), *tartes exotiques* (fruit tarts with kiwi), *tartes au citron*, (lemon tarts), *sablés aux pruneaux et framboises*, (prune and raspberry squares), *têtes de nègre* (chocolate truffles), mostly for €2.30; plus *éclairs* for €2, and most appropriate for the area, *les religieuses* (cream puffs filled with chocolate or coffee cream, with a smaller cream-filled puff on top, iced with chocolate or coffee). If you started your day later than early morning, you may want the *crêpes*, a quiche for €2.60, or one of the wonderful-looking sandwiches of chicken (*poulet*) or ham (*jambon*) for €3.70. Given that it was ten in the morning, Jeanette and Georgette wanted more of a breakfast pastry than a dessert pastry, so they studied their many choices of *croissants, pains aux raisins au chocolat,* and *petit*

Tarte aux Framboises

Sablé (shortbread dough) forms the base for a raspberry mixture made from fresh raspberries steeped in Armagnac that tastes as good as the July raspberries served only in season with heavy cream at the Ritz in Boston. The mixture is topped with a criss-cross pastry and powdered sugar. This is great as a Danish with a morning *café au lait* (tourist and schoolbook expression for a *café crème*)—the only time that the French add milk to their coffee.

variations of breads and rolls, and then selected the *tarte aux framboises.*

With pastry in hand you can go back to point zero, where you mustn't overlook the larger-than-

life statue of Charlemagne on his even larger-than-life horse, which dates from 1882. You can sit on one of the benches circling the statue to eat your pastry. Or if you have small children and want a spot where they can romp safely while you sit on a bench, go to the Square Jean XXIII, a charming little gated park bordering the Seine on the right of Notre-Dame. It's a peaceful place with benches, street lanterns, flowers—a great spot to get away from the overbearing crowd in front of the cathedral.

If you want to walk in the other direction, closest to the pastry shop and away from Notre-Dame, take a few steps to the Pont d'Arcole, which crosses the Seine. Set your pastry on the counter-height wall of the bridge and enjoy eating it in the sun with Parisian river sights of fishermen, male and female bathing beauties in spring and summer, and the *bateaux-mouches* (pleasure boats) year-around.

Before you leave the Cathedral of Notre-Dame area, look up at this magnificent structure, with its double towers and three main doors in front and flying buttresses in back, which took two centuries to build, beginning in 1163. After eating your pastry, you may want to walk it off by climbing the 387 steps up the north tower to see a close-up of the famous gargoyles

*E*ager for coffee after your *tarte aux framboises splendides*, or whatever first pastry you selected, make your way to the nearest café. Keep in mind throughout your *Paris by Pastry* visit that coffee at the bar is half the price of coffee at the table. A black coffee (*un café*) is usually €1.20—check the euro-to-U.S.-dollar rates before you go; if the rate is good for the U.S. dollar, Jeanette thinks you can afford to sit down once in a while to have your coffee. If it's a strong euro, Georgette won't even consider paying €2.40 (double!) for a coffee when she can stand right up at that bar with the Parisians. Coffee on the *terrasse* (sidewalk) is higher still. You may decide that the table is worth the euros because you can have a rest, write postcards, and read your guide to plan your next pastry adventure. Or you may decide the sidewalk is worth the euros to take the sun and watch the people.

Remember, you are *not* going to order a *café au lait*. Ask for *café crème, petit ou grand*, to feel more like a Parisian and less like a tourist. *Café crème* does not mean it is made with cream; it's steamed milk. Or you may prefer *un café, café express,* or *café noir*, all of which mean a black espresso coffee. If the coffee is too strong, ask for a *café allongé*, which will come diluted with hot water. All coffee in France is espresso coffee.

and the spectacular views of Paris. Perhaps you recall reading Victor Hugo's *The Hunchback of Notre-Dame*, written in 1831. It was Victor Hugo who revived the interest in the restoration of this Gothic edifice. Visit its interior to gaze in awe at the priceless rose windows, sculptures, nave, transepts, and altar. If you prefer to see Notre-Dame during an authentic activity rather than on a tour, plan to attend the daily or Sunday services beginning at 8 AM or the free organ concerts on Sundays at 4:45 PM.

Musée du Louvre

Place du Louvre, in the Tuileries, rue St-Honoré, Paris 01
Telephone: 01.40.20.51.51
Metro: Palais Royal, Louvre
Buses: 21, 24, 27, 39, 48, 67, 68, 69, 72, 75, 76, 81, 85, 95
Closed: Tuesdays

Is there any place that attracts more people in Paris than the Louvre? Maybe the Cathedral of Notre-Dame, but that must be it. Just think of it: Paris is the most beautiful city to walk in, with the most glorious architecture, a city built on both sides of a major river with magnificent bridges crossing throughout the city, and no building (except one) above seven stories high, and gardens beyond gardens and fountains and statues. As if that weren't more than any

human being can take in, Paris gives us the Musée du Louvre, containing one of the most important art collections in the world, and built before America was even thought of, in 1190.

The Louvre, in the Tuileries area, is in the 1st arrondissement, the most glamorous quarter of Paris. The 1st arrondissement is bordered by the Place de la Concorde on the west (the American Embassy, five-star hotels, top restaurants, international jewelers are located here in the 1st), the Louvre on the east, by the Seine and the formal gardens of the Tuileries on the south, and rue St-Honoré on the north. Paris was planned so that on a clear day you can stand at the Louvre and see all the way up the avenue des Champs-Elysées to the Arc de Triomphe. Jeanette and Georgette must pay special homage to the Tuileries area because St-Honoré is the patron saint of pastry chefs! *Avec raison* (with reason), as the French would say.

When you arrive at rue St-Honoré you will find chic, sophisticated, outstanding pastry shops to match the famous fashion houses of Chanel, Pierre Cardin, Lanvin, Balmain, Dior, Balenciaga, Givenchy and Hermès. It is from St-Honoré that you will want to select your pastry to eat in the Tuileries gardens, or while waiting in line to enter the Louvre, or

while admiring the statue of Joan of Arc at the Place des Pyramides, or even while studying the architecture of the Comédie Française theatre. You could wait to eat your pastry until you arrive at the Place Colette, or the Royal Palace, or the St-Roch Church, or while visiting the three-floor department store or art galleries and antique shops at the Louvre des Antiquaires. Better still, save your pastry until you can take it easy, going for the essence of Paris and smelling the roses in the Royal Palace garden.

Don't plan on doing this area in one day, however. Jeanette and Georgette know that even the best pastries in the world won't give you enough energy to take it all in.

Go where your heart leads you, never mind what others say you "must see." Always remember while in Paris that "you'll be back"; you don't need to race around to see it all this time. Jeanette usually heads for the boutiques while Georgette heads for the golden statue of Joan of Arc. Then, each with a pastry in hand, they meet in the ticket line of the Louvre, knowing that one pastry will be shared immediately, and the second one a bit later, inside the Louvre, under the pyramid at a little café. There, coffee and ice cream are sold, but the pastries are just too ordinary to even consider.

After you buy your admission ticket, check out all of the hi-tech screens to find out which paintings are where. Just follow the crowd (of course, you will be the only one taking the few stairs—not the escalators—and you know why), up to the Grand Hall of the Denon Wing toward the galleries. You can't miss the *Vénus de Milo,* and, like being at the Taj Mahal, tears will come easily at the sight of this epitome of feminine beauty. Pay special attention to the fine drape over Vénus as you keep in mind that this ever-so-delicate-looking fabric is sculptured in *stone,* and was created at the end of the 2nd century BC. From the Grand Hall, Georgette always makes a point of walking right past the *Mona Lisa,* feeling that anything that popular can't be truly appreciated, to the Rubens room to see the history of Catherine de Médicis. Reading the French phrases beneath each painting (high school French is sufficient!) and looking once again at the giant masterpieces is a thrilling experience. And the Rubens room is never crowded. Not even in July or August.

We start our hunt for a perfect pastry *au Louvre* with

Gargantua
284, rue St-Honoré, Paris 01
Telephone: 01.42.60.52.54
Metro: Palais-Royal, Tuileries
Open: 7 days a week

Two blocks from the metro, the Gargantua has gone from a pâtisserie to much more, to include waiter service for lunch as well as for pastries and chocolates. Nothing below an "8" will be found here! If you take the metro to the Tuileries stop, you will first walk past the gilded statue of Joan of Arc on a horse in full battle regalia in the Place des Pyramides. You will see this striking monument to the woman who attacked the St-Honoré Gate to liberate Paris from the occupying English in 1429. Now walk right up rue des Pyramides to the Gargantua on the corner of St-Honoré. This wonderful pastry haven is also a *salon de thé,* providing a small coffee bar with eight stools in the corner and little tables on the sidewalk for eating its pastries or the magnificent choice of salads and smoked fish that looked good to both Jeanette and Georgette even the first thing in the morning. The *forêt noire* (black forest) for €3.30 looked out of this world. J. *et* G. bought the *St-Honoré* to take to the Louvre, even though the *mille-feuilles* (napoleons) for €2.90 couldn't have looked better and the *sablé* (shortbread) with chocolate mousse appeared delectable.

St-Honoré

A base of *pâte à choux* (puff pastry) is layered with *crème chiboust* and topped with glazed caramel. *Crème chiboust* is made from a pastry custard of egg yolks, flour, sugar, and milk, to which gelatin, butter, eggs, sugar, and a little dark rum have been added. Of course, Jeanette and Georgette buy a single puff to share, but if you are in a group, you can get a cake-plate-sized pastry made up of a ring of puffs. It seemed to J. *et* G. that the *St-Honoré* is a caramel version of the chocolate profiterole. This dessert represents the heavenly crown of St-Honoré; you do remember that he is the patron saint of pastry cooks? J. *et* G. expect *all* of their readers to taste a *St-Honoré* before they leave Paris. It's *de rigueur* of *Paris by Pastry!*

There are so many St-Honoré pâtisseries to try, that Jeanette and Georgette leave the Louvre every two hours for a pastry and coffee treat. This time they decided not to check out the top-of-the-line Gosselin at 123, rue St-Honoré because there is another one near the Musée d'Orsay that they know well. Always stalking the untried and maybe true, they went for

Aux Castelblangeois
Olivier Pottier
168, rue St-Honoré, Paris 0l
Telephone: 01.42.60.77.40
Metro: Tuileries, Palais Royal
Closed: Sundays pm, Mondays

This small, new, modern pâtisserie with a few tables at which to sit down had the longest, quickest, most efficient line near the Louvre. You can look at all the pastries from outside, because once you hit that line, you have to think fast! The *charlotte au chocolat* and *élégance* looked wonderful for €2.80, and the *St-Honoré* is not to be missed for €1.90. Other puff pastries—*religieuses, divorcées*, and *éclairs*—were all bigger than usual for €2, a *pain au chocolat* that looked like a chocolate *madeleine* was €1.80, and they even had a *beignet* (doughnut) for €1.20. For the first time, J. *et* G. saw a *mogador Grand Marnier* that looked like a chocolate-covered hot dog on a stick. Actually, it was a chocolate-flavored sponge cake laced with Grand Marnier (an orange liqueur made in France) and dusted all around with cocoa. Besides pastries, it's the salads "to go" for €4 and the great variety of sandwiches that the nearby workers come in to buy that make it a long, fast line.

What to choose? The *arlequin*, which is a three-layer chocolate-almond sponge cake flavored with scotch, with alternate layers of dark chocolate and white chocolate mousse. Or the *lippizaner*, which is another chocolate-almond sponge-cake base, but this one is topped with a light, cherry-studded chocolate mousse. Whole cherries covered the top of the chocolate icing. J. *et* G. hit Aux Castelblangeois at 4 PM, ready to sit at one of those sidewalk tables and enjoy the prettiest pastry they had ever seen in all of Paris: *la princesse.* This one was an oval-shaped pastry dressed in a thin layer of pale green marzipan, topped with a real rose. Exquisite. Their art-weary bodies and overloaded minds were jump-started just by looking at this pastry. There were three layers of buttery sponge cake soaked in gin-raspberry syrup and filled with a smooth custard cream. When Jeanette asked about the custard cream and learned that it contained gin, Georgette decided to call it a day and go straight home

after their coffee to mix a good old American dry martini to cut through the hard day's work of rich pastry-tasting.

Jardin du Luxembourg
Boulevard St-Michel, Paris 06
Telephone: 01.42.34.20.00
Metro: St-Michel, Vavin
Closed: April–Oct. 9 pm;
Nov.–March 5 pm

If you could choose anywhere in the whole wide world, where would you go for your fiftieth birthday? Georgette chose Paris and the Jardin du Luxembourg (Luxembourg Gardens), hands down. Back when she studied French in high school, she thought the Luxembourg Gardens sounded like the best part of Paris. Arriving for the first time as a junior in college, she spent many hours in the green chairs—looking, listening, tasting, and smelling the thrill of Paris. Arriving in Paris every year, Jeanette and Georgette don't feel at home until they have carried their picnic, with pastry (*bien sûr*—of course) to their favorite spot. With their backs to Montparnasse (the only skyscraper in Paris, it broke the building code to rise 56 floors—690 feet—to offend the rest of the city), J. *et* G. face the gardens, statues, and model boat pond, and just watch the families parading through.

They always check the band-concert schedule posted on the bandstand toward boulevard St-Michel ("boul' Mich'," as the French students call it) and so far have never been to Paris without attending a 3 PM concert in the Luxembourg Gardens. Here is one place that Jeanette knows Sainte-Geneviève (patron saint of Paris) oversees the Gardens. (Georgette still isn't sure of the statue on the bridge going to Ile St-Louis.)

J. *et* G. usually enter the gardens by way of metro Vavin, just so they can walk down rue Vavin and look up at the boarding house where Jeanette lived during the winter she studied at the Sorbonne. Underneath the *pension* is a café facing the gardens, and on rue Vavin the many pastry shops that used to be there are now turned into children's shops. Entering the gardens from rue Vavin, you will walk by the beekeeping school and see the agriculture department's grafting of fruit trees which are later planted all over Paris. You will also see the reproduction of the Statue of Liberty. And don't miss the statues of Sainte-Geneviève, French queens, and 19th-century women standing amongst the busts of the poets, philosophers and French writers. Georgette always studies in the gardens right after her classes at the Alliance Française (trying to learn some French on her own so that Jeanette doesn't have to teach her

everything) before meeting her learned pal later in the day. And during a heat wave, the only cool resting place that Georgette knows in Paris is at the Fontaine de Médicis, the 17th-century Italian grotto. It is draped with greens, beautified by columns topped with stone vases of impatiens, and shaded by a thicket of trees lining the goldfish pool, beside which the Parisians sit in a row reflecting on the beauty of the Luxembourg Gardens. Pony rides, tricycle races, and a tennis court (where Georgette often plays tennis) are the active ingredients of this thrilling place.

Now is the time that Georgette must give her little lecture on the "unfriendly French," by American standards. She developed her theory here at the Luxembourg Gardens. You will notice that even when the French are together with friends (and many people come by themselves to sit, meditate, read, smoke, and admire the flowers, trees, lawns, and natural beauty), if they speak at all, it is in hushed tones. It reminds Georgette of the behavior we Americans expect in a library. But in Paris, this library behavior is outdoors! In a park. Therefore, if the French don't even speak to each other because they respect their own and their companions' privacy so much, it's no wonder that they aren't looking at foreigners, ready to leap in with chit-chat or conversation, *oui, d'accord?* For example, a radio would be unthinkable in the Gardens! This is a very different culture. Parks are sanctuaries. You can *not* walk, sit, or—heaven forbid—sunbathe on the grass! In any Parisian park. *Non, une exception!* In the Parc Monceau, there is one very small, 10-by-30-foot fenced-off area with a sign that says if you are with children under three, you may walk and play on the grass. See what Georgette means? The French are different, not unfriendly. They give priority to privacy and quiet even among themselves, nothing to do with friendly or not toward Americans.

Ah, oui! A pastry. On the corner of rue Vavin and rue Notre-Dame-des-Champs you will see

**Boulangerie-Pâtisserie
Au Pain du Vavin**
*54, rue Notre-Dame-des-Champs,
Paris 06
Telephone: 01.43.54.99.54
Metro: Vavin
Closed: Sundays*

Here is the only pâtisserie in the area at which to buy your "9" and "10" pastries or sandwiches to carry to the Jardin du Luxembourg. Exit from the metro on rue Delambre and walk down Montparnesse to Vavin. On your right you will find this modern, chic shop and its narrow marble counter with stools on which to have a coffee if you just can't wait to take your *pâtisserie* to

the gardens. A very fine place and open on Monday! Very modern-looking. Jeanette and Georgette were taken aback when they went into this shop, thinking they were back in NYC instead of Paris. One of the few new pastry shops in the *quartier,* it had better receive the J. *et* G. test! *Et chic, alors,* they selected the most luscious little chocolate cupcake that has ever been created . . .

*Gâteau au
Chocolat
Pistache*

Made with bitter chocolate, this cylinder-shaped *gâteau au chocolat* had a soft, creamy pistachio sauce surrounding a white-chocolate center. Sprinkled with chopped pistachio nuts, it was served warm with a mound of almond-flavored whipped cream on the side. Worth a trip to Paris? You bet!

Of course you are going to enjoy the leisure of the Luxembourg Gardens most by bringing your pastry with you. If you are entering the gardens, however, by the boul' Mich' side of the park, then get off the metro at St-Michel and walk up the boulevard, where you will find one of the most elegant groups of pastry shops in Paris, with an upstairs tea room, but you'll want a pastry to go, *bien sûr*.

Dalloyau
2, Place Edmond Rostand,
Paris 06
Telephone: 01.43.29.31.10
Metro: St-Michel
Closed: Jamais—never!

Let's just stand and look for a few minutes. Don't hurry that pastry choice! See the *riz impératrice?* The *crème brûlée russe?* The *mousse au chocolat gingembre?* The *coupe à l'orange?* The *crème caramel aux noisettes?* Here is the place to see what is, not necessarily to spend and eat. As Georgette says, "We don't have to want or have everything we see, and it's always good to know what our options are." For €5 (*très cher*), Jeanette chose the *marron au cassis*, a pastry based on a sponge layer, topped with a cream-cheese-and-*cassis* (black currant) mixture, and finished with a glaze of caramelized *marron* (chestnut) that

tasted to J. *et* G. like butterscotch. Everything in the showcase looked like an award-winning pastry. You can go upstairs to the tea room if it is raining or you want to eat lunch before you carry your pastry to a band concert or to a green chair in the gardens. J. *et* G. saved their after-pastry coffee until their walk back to the metro. They crossed boul' Mich' and walked down two blocks to the Place de la Sorbonne, where they often take their coffee at the Tabac de la Sorbonne, Jeanette's old haunt near the university where she studied. Here is the best example of Parisian pricing: a coffee on the terrace in front of the café is €4.20, a coffee at a table in the first interior (under a roof, like a porch) is €2.40, *but* a coffee standing at the "zinc"—where even in July, J. *et* G. were the only non-Parisians (as much as they hate to admit that they weren't born and raised in Paris)—is €1.20!

Champs-Elysées
Avenue des Champs-Elysées,
Paris, 08
Metro: Charles de Gaulle, Etoile

Who doesn't take a walk on the Champs-Elysées the first thing, as soon as they arrive in Paris? Whether to marvel at the perspective from the Arc de Triomphe to the Louvre, or to check on tickets for the season's blockbuster art show in the Grand Palais, or to window-shop to see the latest watches, French cosmetics, and designer fountain pens, or to see what the new Louis Vuitton shop looks like, or to look in the Renault, Mercedes-Benz, and Toyota showrooms (and Citroën coming soon in a futuristic, glass building of its own), or to check out the latest cinemas, or to look across to the Pont Alexandre III, or to go to the post office, or to marvel at the gardens, fountains, and flower beds along the way, or to just sit down at a sidewalk café to see who's in town—there are as many reasons to walk the Champs-Elysées as there are kinds of people for each of those reasons.

If you get overwhelmed and need a ten-minute break of peace and quiet, make your way to the Renault showroom, 53, avenue Champs-Elysées, and there you will find a special car exhibit (which was on race cars during a recent visit), a futuristic, modern, super-clean restroom, four big cushions in the showroom to sit on, and newspapers for you to read including the British *Daily Telegraph*, the Italian *la Republico*, the German *Die Welt*, several French newspapers, and even *USA Today*.

To begin your adventure, take the metro to Place Charles de Gaulle, Etoile. There are many exits but it is most fun and dramatic to follow the exit signs for *Champs-Elysées (Arc de Triomphe)*. Jeanette instructs us that "Champs-Elysées" means "the dwelling place of the most happy" in ancient mythology. She told Georgette that this "triumphal way," as the French call it, all started with Marie de Médicis, who turned the world's most well-known boulevard into a fashionable carriage-drive in the early 15th century. It is the two-mile avenue from the Place de la Concorde (where the U.S. Embassy is located), which is marked by the 3,300-year-old granite Egyptian obelisk, to Napoleon's Arc de Triomphe, which describes all of his triumphs in battle sculptures. This is where the Tour de France finishes its annual bicycle race, and where the Bastille Day parade marches every year.

Whatever your reason for going there, you will not find a pâtisserie on the Champs-Elysées. Oh yes, you will see chains such as La Broche Dorée, all kinds of fast food places, plenty of very ordinary snacks. But they are like a one-star hotel when searching the four-star, or a "12" Zagat rating when your standards of excellence are nothing under a "20"! We are not looking to fill up on sweets; *mais non*, we are searching for the best of pastries, the Parisian best!

J. *et* G. searched high and low, east and west, to find the best and

Mottier
Pâtisserie des Champs-Elysées

28, rue Washington, Paris 08
Telephone: 01.42.56.00.66
Metro: Charles de Gaulle, FDR
Closed: Sundays, Mondays

Very small and traditional, Mottier is an "artisan" shop as opposed to a chain pastry shop. Usually family owned, artisan pâtisseries are always privately owned, and Georgette, the American capitalist, always prefers individual pride in a pastry shop over corporate ownership, of course.

The *pain aux raisins*, €1, looked custard-creamy; the *tarte aux poires* and *religieuse* (€2.30 to €2.40) were enticing. The *religieuse* is a favorite of Georgette's brother John, who lives in the Netherlands and always comes down to Paris to help out J. *et* G. with their pastry-tasting, and who was with us on this morning to start the day. There are five stools and a narrow counter for rainy days, or for those needing a respite before tackling the rest of the Champs-Elysées. We decided to take the *pain aux raisins* to eat right away, and save the *religieuse* for the first bench on the Champs to watch the people go by.

Then it was on down toward the Franklin D. Roosevelt metro station, just below the George V stop where Georgette wanted to

closest pastry shop. They hunted something delectable to take to the cinema to eat at intermission time. They wanted to set an example for the quality pastry that they know their dear readers wandering on this boulevard deserve. So. Because we never settle for less, we started walking down the left sidewalk from the Arc de Triomphe until we came to Washington Street. (You, of course, will be enjoying the sights and people on the Champs-Elysées as you walk—not searching for a pastry, because J. *et* G. have already found your pâtisserie.) Take a left and keep walking right by the chain of Mi Do Ré until you are almost at the end of the street, and you find show John the magnificent 1913 art-nouveau Guerlain Building at 68, Champs-Elysées, one of three national monument houses left on the boulevard. Guerlain, a family-owned business, created one of the world's three best-selling perfumes, Shalimar, which is almost a hundred years old. Jeanette *et* Georgette always walk across the Champs-Elysées to admire the complete look of the splendid stucco ornaments, the wrought-iron balconies across the bowed windows, and the brass fixtures, before they walk into the sales room of white marble and wood paneling. This time Georgette thought it looked much smaller and was told that they were renovating the sales room to expand to the first floor. (Of course our dear readers know that the French do not count the ground floor as the first; that is the ground zero, and first floor is one up.)

The Champs-Elysées is the place to stroll, to stop and see the old amongst the new, the Renault car museum beside the fast-food sidewalk restaurants. On a beautiful day, you will keep walking down from Guerlain until you come toward the Grand Palais on your right at Franklin D. Roosevelt. Of course you will already have checked *L'Officiel* to find what art exhibit is being shown while you are in Paris. If

you are coming from another direction to the Grand Palais, take the metro to Franklin D. Roosevelt, come out of the metro, and walk a block across the Champs away from the Palais. Take a right on rue de Ponthieu and continue half a block to the corner of 5, rue de Ponthieu and rue Jean Mermoz to find

La Gerbe d'Or
5, rue Ponthieu and rue Jean Mermoz, Paris 08
Metro: Franklin D. Roosevelt
Closed: Saturdays, Sundays

La Gerbe d'Or sells the only outstanding pastries on the lower half of the Champs-Elysées. Hard to believe until you realize that the pâtisseries are mainly in the residential areas of Paris, not in the commercial and tourist areas. Stopping at a pâtisserie is part of the daily shopping to take home, along with purchases from the butcher, the vegetable market, the *fromagerie* (for cheese and butter), and the wine store. The French who work nearby on the Champs-Elysées buy their lunch, sandwiches, and pastries at this tea salon. You will not be disappointed at this busy, narrow shop filled with a selection of pastries that appeared to be at least an "8," with a counter and high stools if you want to eat your sandwich and take a coffee there.

Jeanette and Georgette were on their way to the Grand Palais and, as always, planned to take a pastry break with an after-pastry coffee at the Grand Palais. The coffee is always good, but the pastries are too uneventful for the event. Experienced as they are, they selected a chocolate pastry, a wedge of the *richelieu* to take to the art treat of the season.

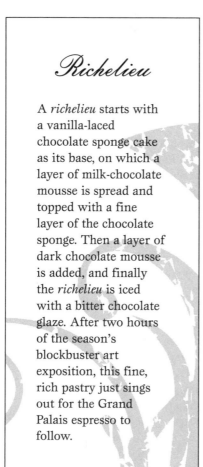

Richelieu

A *richelieu* starts with a vanilla-laced chocolate sponge cake as its base, on which a layer of milk-chocolate mousse is spread and topped with a fine layer of the chocolate sponge. Then a layer of dark chocolate mousse is added, and finally the *richelieu* is iced with a bitter chocolate glaze. After two hours of the season's blockbuster art exposition, this fine, rich pastry just sings out for the Grand Palais espresso to follow.

Musée d'Orsay
1, rue de Bellechasse, Paris 07
Telephone: 01.40.49.48.14
Metro: Solférino
Closed: Mondays

You won't have to know art to go to this most popular of museums. It is the old Orsay railroad station, turned museum in 1986 to house the Impressionists' paintings, and all of the art that belongs between the medieval art of the Louvre and the modern art of the Pompidou Center. Here in this historical landmark on the Seine you will find Jeanette's favorites of Manet, Renoir, Degas, and Van Gogh, and Georgette's favorites of Bonnard and Vuillard, Redon and Rousseau. With all the outstanding 7th-arrondissement pâtisseries described later in *Paris by Pastry* (see "The Pastry Hunt" chapter in particular), you might think that you will never need another pastry shop in the 7th, but J. *et* G. can't resist one more because (a) it's so close to the Musée d'Orsay, and (b) it simply should not be missed!

Gosselin
258, boulevard Saint-Germain, Paris 07
Telephone: 01.45.51.53.11
Metro: Solférino
Closed: Sundays

Take the escalator *sortie* from the metro stop and you will be right at

---

Valencia Cake

A base of chocolate-almond sponge cake is soaked in orange syrup made of syrup, orange juice concentrate, and vodka; a light gelatin custard of cream, fresh orange juice, and butter fills the flan ring over the cake. Another layer of orange-soaked chocolate-almond sponge cake goes on top. After it is chilled, the pastry is decorated with candied orange peel and shards of chocolate, placed as close together as possible.

---

the door of Gosselin! It is only two blocks from the Musée d'Orsay, where it's best to eat your pastry on the steps watching the artsy street action. Parisians flock to the Gosselin for family-size tarts and cakes. The *pains aux raisins* are a "10+" at €1.80, the *mille-feuilles* creamy and oozing at €2.10, and if you are planning a picnic lunch on the steps of the Orsay, then consider the sandwiches from this pâtisserie. The choices are few and the lines are long inside the museum. Unlike the Louvre, the food isn't as well organized at the Orsay, according to J. *et* G., and who is more interested in your eating satisfaction while in Paris than Jeanette *et* Georgette?

Tour Eiffel

Champ-de-Mars, Paris 07
Telephone: 01.45.50.34.56
Metro: Ecole-Militaire,
Bir Hakeim
RER: Champ-de-Mars
Bus: 42, 69, 72, 82

To many travelers, La Tour Eiffel *is* Paris! Back in 1889 it was considered bizarre and extremely ugly, although it was designed to enhance the technical age of Thomas Edison and Alexander Graham Bell. After years of ingratiating itself into the Paris skyline, it has grown into a real landmark beauty in the eyes of many French as well as tourists. The Eiffel Tower is open April

through October from 9 AM to 11 PM, November to March from 9:30 AM to 11 PM, and in July and August from 9 AM to midnight. There is a small museum, the Cinémax, at its base which tells the history of the Tour Eiffel through a short film, including famous personalities who have visited there. During the tourist season, the double-decker elevators can take up to two hours to reach the top. Once on the highest level, 800 people can stay there at one time, and the tower is constructed so that the 10,100 tons of metal never sway more than 4 inches!

Those of you who are serious about your pastries will want to take the 1,652 steps to the third level of the tower at 899 feet, so that you will build your appetite for the delectable treats below or for the ones that you carry to eat at the top. Others of you who may settle on sharing a pastry, can plan less exercise and take the 360 steps to the first level at 187 feet. Or if you just don't care how little exercise you get, you can take the elevator. It is said that from the top, you can see 45 miles away to Chartres Cathedral, outside of Paris.

If you want to stay away from the hub of the tourist scene, just find your way to 21, avenue de la Bourdonnais, which borders the Tour Eiffel on the east. Unlike some other tourist attractions in Paris, this is a swell neighborhood: no souvenir shops, commercial stands, or street vendors selling watches, knock-off Louis Vuitton

Puits d'Amour

A *puits d'amour* is as heavenly as its name. The "well of love," or "wishing well," is made from a *pâte à choux* (cream puff pastry) used mainly for the *éclair,* the *paris-brest,* the *St-Honoré,* and the *profiterole.* It is less fragile and rich than *pâte sablée* (shortbread pastry) but richer than a *pâte à foncer* (lining pastry). The puff, about a three-inch round, is filled with *crème chiboust,* a mixture of *crème pâtissière* (basic pastry custard of egg yolks, sugar, flour, milk, and vanilla) and *meringue italienne.* The combination presents a light, creamy, delicious custard-cream that is pure ambrosia.

bags, or flying tin birds. In this elegant residential section of Paris, the best pastry shop is where the French come for their daily pastries. You will easily find the La Tour Eiffel pastry shop only a half-block from the base of the tower with an exquisite array of pastries.

Boulangerie-Pâtisserie de La Tour Eiffel
F. Fegueux
21, avenue de La Bourdonnais, Paris 07
Telephone: 01.47.05.59.81
Metro: Champ-de-Mars
Closed: August

You can buy a pastry to take with you and eat while you are standing in line to go to the top of the tower, or you can sit at one of the few tables outside the shop, or you may prefer to sit inside and look at the expansive lattice-work of the Tour Eiffel. You can also buy, "to go" (*à emporter*), exceptional baguette sandwiches (*crudités,* chicken, cheese), and there is a glass-front refrigerator with Cokes, water, and orange soda for €3. The pastry showcase, beveled mirror, seasonal window of Easter eggs, fish, bells, and chocolate bunnies, beautiful fresh flowers on the counter, and the blond paneled wood will come together to remind you that you are in Paris, where aesthetics are highly valued in the daily life of French culture. You will find the pastries all an "8" or above at this shop. Not tasted, the *fraise* (strawberry) and *abricot* (apricot) tarts looked fabulous, although G. would say that the *poire* (pear) tart was probably a perfect "10" at €2.50. J. *et* G. also pondered the lemon tart with a soft meringue and caramelized glaze, the *sablé* (shortbread cookie) glazed and topped with raisins, the chocolate tart, the *baba au rhum,* and of course, the *mille-feuilles* (napoleons)—one with a perfect-looking custard-cream oozing out of the puff pastry and topped with a chocolate drizzled glaze, another with a vanilla frosting, and the best of all, the one with a powdered-sugar topping. The *éclairs* and the *religieuses* looked awfully good, and a new pastry to J. *et* G. was the *trois chocolats,* three small puffs in a triangle— one each of dark chocolate, mild chocolate, and white chocolate with cocoa sprinkled on top for €3.50. New to them also was the *courchevel,* a *crêpe* draped over a

pastry round and glazed with syrup; but because it was frosted all around with a thick icing, it was too much for that moment.

Jeanette and Georgette decided they had to stop eating their favorite fruit tarts and chocolate *éclairs* all the time and should start trying new pastries if they were going to be serious about describing Paris by pastry. And so it was here, at the Pâtisserie de La Tour Eiffel, that they had their first taste of paradise. Easily a "9" was the thrilling *puits d'amour.*

This pâtisserie was so good, that J. *et* G. returned within a week to take Georgette's brother (chocolate torte with hazelnuts layered with chocolate cream, and topped with cocoa), her first cousin once removed (raspberry mousse filled with whole fresh raspberries between a shortbread cake topped with powdered sugar), and her fiancé (a flavorful fresh-pear tart with whipped cream and meringue) to share their luscious find!

Recipe for Puits d'Amour

After describing the *puits d'amour*, Jeanette told Georgette that it just won't do . . . their dear readers must have the recipe. After all, some may want to make that "well of love" in America, and a description, no matter how accurate, will hardly do for baking it at home. And so, once again, Georgette paid attention to Jeanette's advice. Here it is, not simple, a recipe in three parts for ten *puits. Ooh, là là!*

Part 1
Pâte à Choux
 1/4 cup, plus one tablespoon of water
 1 tablespoon of sweet (unsalted) butter
 1/4 teaspoon salt
 1/4 teaspoon sugar
 1/4 cup flour
 1 egg

In a medium saucepan, heat water, butter, salt and sugar to a boil. Remove from heat and add flour all at once, then stir until a stiff, slightly lumpy dough is formed. Return to heat and cook for 1 minute, stirring constantly with a wooden spoon, until dough pulls away from sides of pan and forms a ball.

Turn the hot dough into a large mixing bowl, and beat in the egg until well blended. While the *pâte* is cooling, the Parisian pastry chefs prepare the *crème chiboust.* Georgette, on the other hand, gets her little *choux* all baked *and* caramelized before she even thinks of preparing the *crème chiboust!* Be sure the pastry puffs are all set to go when your chiboust is ready.

Preheat the oven to 375°F. Brush a 10-muffin tin with melted butter. Drop 1 heaping teaspoon of *pâte à choux* into each cup, and with a wet finger, spread *pâte* around to line the cups as evenly as possible. Place in oven, keeping oven door open a crack with a potholder or wooden spoon and bake for 20 minutes, until golden brown. Remove from oven, press down centers, and cool.

Part 2
Crème Chiboust

Chiboust cream is a light pastry cream mixed with an Italian meringue. Everything must be done rapidly, so have all of your ingredients together before you begin. The chiboust cream must be used as soon as possible after it is prepared. It also must be eaten on the same day. But that's the easy part!

Making the pastry cream:

1/3 cup sugar
2 tablespoons flour
Pinch of salt
1 cup milk
3 egg yolks
1/4 teaspoon vanilla extract

Place the milk in a medium saucepan and bring to a boil. Cover and keep hot. With the wire whisk, beat the sugar and egg yolks together until the mixture whitens and forms a ribbon; then slowly stir in the flour and salt with the whisk. Pour the hot milk into the egg-and-sugar mixture, beating all constantly with the wire whisk. Pour the mixture back into the saucepan and bring to a boil again, stirring constantly with the wire whisk so that the mixture does not stick to the bottom of the saucepan. Boil for 1 minute, stirring vigorously, then pour into a bowl, stir in the vanilla, and lightly rub the surface of the cream with a lump of butter to keep a skin from forming as it cools.

Making the meringue:
1/3 cup (scant) granulated sugar
2 tablespoons water
4 egg whites
5 teaspoons granulated sugar

Place the 1/3 cup of sugar with the water in a small saucepan. Bring to a boil, stirring until the sugar is dissolved. As the sugar cooks, beat the whites until very stiff, adding the 5 teaspoons of sugar halfway through. This takes about 5 minutes. Monitor the temperature of the boiling sugar. When it reaches 248°F, the hard-ball stage, it is ready to use. With the mixer on high speed, pour the boiling sugar into the egg whites, being careful not to let it fall on the edge of the bowl or on the beaters.

Putting it together:
Using a whisk, stir one-third of the meringue into the warm pastry cream, then, with a spatula, gently fold in the rest until the mixture is completely homogenous. Do not overwork, or the cream, like temperamental love, will collapse, and this is suppose to be a very light mixture!

Are your caramelized *pâte à choux* puffs ready to go? Oh no! The recipe for the caramel part . . .

Part 3
Caramel
1 cup sugar
4 tablespoons water
1 teaspoon lemon juice

In a medium saucepan, stir together the sugar, water, and lemon juice, and cook over medium heat until the mixture begins to bubble. Lower the heat and continue cooking. When the sugar begins to darken, tilt the pan slightly in a rotating motion so that it will color evenly. Don't stir. When the caramel has taken on a deep amber color, it's ready to use.

Immediately take the *pâte à choux* shells and, holding them upside down, dip the rims in the hot caramel. Turn right side up and cool; the caramel will harden immediately. Phew!

Now. Let's go back to the *crème chiboust* and put it all together. Carefully spoon the pastry cream into each puff, or do as the French do: spoon it into a pastry bag and fill the shells using a swirling motion. Wait—one more step. Sprinkle the filled pastries with sugar and place them on a baking sheet under the broiler for about 1 minute or until the sugar is caramelized. Refrigerate until serving. Serve the same day. Be sure to serve at room temperature! None of this American style of serving from refrigerator to table stuff!

Have a drink! Relax after all of that hard work until the appreciative company arrives.

The Pastry Hunt
Stalking the Delicious

Every state in America has hunting and fishing laws, regulations, and customs. For example, in the *Vermont Digest of Fish & Wildlife Laws*, you can find the length of season, the legal hunting or fishing method, the minimum size, and the daily limit of game or fish for each season. For instance, it says that the deer season is from November 11 to 26. "One deer with at least one antler no less than three inches long may be taken on the hunting license. A firearm or bow and arrow may be used. Shooting hours are one half

hour before sunrise to one half hour after sunset. A person shall not take a swimming deer from any lake, pond, river or other body of water."

Over the years of stalking traditional pastries and trapping the rare species (the Parisians' neighborhood pâtisseries), Jeanette and Georgette have learned the customs and habits of the French pastry-hunters. First of all, *tous* (all) Parisians have a license and pastry-hunting skills. Second, the only legal method for stalking, catching, trapping, and bagging pastries, is by purchasing them with euros. Third, the Parisian law says there is an "open season" which means no closed season, but on the other hand, J. *et* G. have found that Sunday afternoons, Mondays, and the month of August might as well be a closed season, because most pâtisseries are closed on those days. There is no law against buying pastries at any hour, although most shops close for lunch from 1 PM until 3 PM and for the evening at 7 PM. However, Jeanette and Georgette, the original pastry-stalkers, located a few pâtisseries open twenty-four hours a day, seven days a week!

There is no minimum length or weight for pastries captured on the hunt. There is no law stating a daily limit. However, once again, Jeanette and Georgette have learned that for most pastry-hunters, there is a limit of consumption. While the consumption limit of J. *et* G. is no more than one-half a pastry every two hours from 7 AM to 9 PM, they realize that some people are bigger and younger (none walk more!) than they, and perhaps those hunters may want to double the limit, providing themselves with one whole pastry every two hours. Habit and individual custom will be more important than law on this aspect of the pastry hunt. There are also those hunters who would rather shoot the pastry by

camera than to trap it by eating. Again, it will be an individual matter of custom and habit. Whatever your interest in "The Pastry Hunt: Stalking the Delicious," Jeanette *et* Georgette have created a list of

Essential Hunting Gear
1. *Paris by Pastry*, one copy
2. *Carte orange* (transportation license), available by week or month
3. Map of Paris
4. Bottle of water
5. Discerning eye
6. *Bon appétit*
7. Well-sharpened scent sense
8. Bottle of adventurous spirits
9. Curious taste buds
10. Decision-making skills
11. Comfortable shoes

The first trip for beginning pastry-hunters will take you to the 13th arrondissement to learn how to spot the signs, sniff the scent, feel the anticipation of the catch, and devour the trophy. Now who in the world do you know who has ever started out their exploration of Paris in the 13th? *Paris by Pastry* will make a professional Paris explorer and champion pastry-hunter out of you, while your amateur friends get their just desserts only in restaurants!

Pâtisserie Sainte-Anne
193, rue de Tolbiac, Paris 13

Telephone: 01.45.89.59.11
Metro: Tolbiac
Closed: Tuesdays, Wednesdays
Ouverture *(open!)* sans
(without) interruption 7 am to
8 pm

Non, Le Moulin des Prés, also on
Tolbiac is not it! Even though the
traditional painted tiles of bakers
and wheat at that corner
boulangerie-pâtisserie are
traditional and interesting, you are
hunting the best trophies, and you
will not be disappointed when you
finally get to Sainte-Anne!

Delivering a gift for Carol
Scheer, an American friend, to an
address where they had never been
or heard of, Jeanette and Georgette
eagerly accepted their fate to look
for the providential pastry shop on
the corner of rue de l'Espérance
(hope) and rue de la Providence
(divine foresight) when they came
upon this beautiful little pastry
shop, one of the very few that are
open on Mondays. Jeanette spotted
a handsome church, Ste-Anne de la
Maison, standing isolated on a
little isle at the corner of Tolbiac
and Charles Fourier, right across
from the pâtisserie. The shop was
filled with exquisite pastries,
including a wonderful-looking *tarte
princesse aux poires* (puff pastry
layered with fresh stewed pears,
covered with a cream and
meringue combination, topped
with a meringue, and decorated

*Charlotte aux
Framboises*

In America, we usually
make a charlotte with
ladyfingers; in Paris, they
are made with a thin layer
of sponge cake lining each
individual serving. The
filling is a combination of
whipped cream, meringue,
fresh fruit, and gelatin. The
pastry is refrigerated until
solid, and then topped with
a thin layer of sponge cake
and sprinkled with
powdered sugar. Eating this
delectable culinary creation
on the steps of Sainte-
Anne, looking out at this
new neighborhood,
Jeanette and Georgette
were amazed that no
matter where their pastry
hunt takes them in Paris,
pastry and visual treasures
are most definitely to be
found.

with caramelized rosettes), a *tarte
coup de soleil* (a pear cream with
pear liqueur in a pastry, topped
with meringue), a *tarte au citron*

(lemon tart—a lemon custard in a pastry shell topped with a sliver-thin slice of lemon; notice whether there is a thin layer of gelatin covering the lemon mixture—it's best without it), a *gâteau au chocolat américain* (chocolate cake sprinkled with cocoa), and all kinds of fruit tarts. J. *et* G. didn't resist the *charlotte aux framboises* (raspberry charlotte) to carry across the street to the steps of Sainte-Anne.

Paris pastries have even more going than the magnificent shops, the anticipation of the taste during the hunt, the excitement of the selection, the satisfaction of the taste—just wait, dear reader, until you experience the aesthetics of the wrapping! You will know you are in a European culture when you watch your individual pastry being prepared to take with you. The wrapping paper will be folded in such a way that it looks like an upside-down cone—no tape is used, no staples, no bag, sometimes a string on top to carry it with; otherwise you just carry it by the tip of the top. Once you have carried your own wrapped pastry away to your beautiful spot for eating, you will begin to notice the French carrying their pastries home or to the park. You want to know and feel the French culture? Then you must know the sight on the street of the cone-shaped, wrapped pastry. Forget the Tour Eiffel—watching your Paris pastry being wrapped *is* Paris!

Place de la Contrescarpe
Au Nègre Joyeux

Just by happenstance, Jeanette and Georgette arrived at this small, charming square with a fountain in the center surrounded by zinnias in the spring and summer, a green hedge in the winter, and a draped chain on which to sit and eat a pastry. From the hearty pastry shop (**M. Brusa**) on the square at 18, rue Mouffetard, one can get a *charlotte* crowded with huge wedges of pear. In fact, this shop serves big portions of everything—*meringue au chocolat, tête de nègre* (chocolate truffle), very beautiful *tartes tatin* and *chiboutz*. Austrian-type pastries. (Large pastries almost always are your clue that students are nearby, and indeed students gather at dusk and on weekends in this square.) J. *et* G. were more surprised when they came out, looked above the shop, and saw a huge window painting of a French-African standing at a table in front of a lace-curtained window serving wine to Madame at the *Maison fondeé* in 1748. Georgette asked a Parisian to tell her the story of this fascinating treasure and learned that the Place de la Contrescarpe was laid out in 1852 with the

window painting of *Au Nègre Joyeux* in honor of the French 16th-century "pine-cone club," which was a French-African club immortalized in the writings of Rabelais. Jeanette read Rabelais years ago and Georgette tried to catch up recently with *Gargantua* and *Pantagruel.* Look up! Don't miss this unique portrait on glass! It's worth the walk.

Jeanette and Georgette were so excited by this charming little square and window that they didn't get the address. The Place was so small that they couldn't find it on the map, nor even in the official *Taride Paris par Arrondissement.* So. On their very next trip to Paris, they had to retrace their steps and, much to their disappointment, found in

French (of course!) a note: "Following the explosion of our oven, we inform our good customers that the pâtisserie will be closed for an undetermined amount of time. Thank you for your understanding."

They looked around for another pâtisserie, not wanting to leave this delightful Place de la Contrescarpe; it was a real find for their adventuresome readers. They noticed that Häagen-Dazs had many locations in Paris, and this was one of them. Because there was no Ben and Jerry's around (Georgette is a Vermonter and has ten shares of Ben and Jerry's stock), they debated for a long time before deciding to get an ice cream cone from a rival *glacier.* They soon learned and want to warn their readers that a cone "to go" saves you a euro! So don't just sit there; get your ice cream—or pastry, that is, of course, when M. Brusa's ovens are repaired—and carry it just one block away, up rue Blainville, to the corner of rue Thouin. There you will find double green benches and Parisian lampposts surrounded by a little circle of shade trees. You will spot the French sitting there outside of their apartments, and not an American in sight? even in July? except Jeanette *et* Georgette, *bien sûr!*

La Rétrodor
16, rue Mouffetard, Paris 05
Telephone: 01.47.07.06.36
Metro: Place Monge
Closed: Sundays

Jeanette had noticed a specialty bread shop at the Place de la Contrescarpe that she wanted to cite in *Paris by Pastry,* but Georgette said, *non,* if we start adding bread shops, it will be a bread guide to Paris! Finally Jeanette said she would pay for one of the specialties, the *pain aux pommes* (apple bread), and so of course, Jeanette won out once again. If you want a *plaisir, pain aux pommes,* or a *clafoutis aux pommes* (apple custard tart), you can call it a pastry, and find it at La Rétrodor.

So, look up for the painting on

glass of the French-African standing at a table in front of a laced curtain, get your pastry or ice cream or specialty bread "to go" *(merci à Jeanette),* and if it's summer, head for the shade and this truly authentic neighborhood.

Rich Hunting Grounds: The 7th Arrondissement

There are so many reasons to be in the 7th arrondissement, that Jeanette wanted to make sure that you had enough shops to try a different pastry for every occasion when you are visiting the Tour Eiffel, the Esplanade des Invalides, the French Legion of Honor—which is right next to the Musée d'Orsay (which houses the major collection of 19th-century art)—or the Musée Rodin. It is in the 7th that you can walk across the Seine via the most ornate bridge in all of Paris, the Pont Alexandre III. (You may want to eat your pastry on a bench below the bridge at river level.) From the bridge itself, you can see the Eiffel Tower, the American Church of Paris, and the gilded top of the Dôme Church at the Invalides, which houses Napoleon's Tomb.

You will read in the "Seine-à-Seine" chapter about the surprises on Stop #7, rue Vaneau. A surprise to match almost any surprise is also in the 7th arrondissement when you look at the window of

Deyrolle at 46, rue du Bac, and see clothes and hats being sold in a taxidermist shop with shirts on deer, hats on bears, and many more surprises than one arrondissement should hold. You can see that the 7th is a serious place, even though there are a lot of outstanding pastry shops—you will need them for the countless 7th sights and prize Parisian attractions you find there. Besides the usual places, Georgette always hurries off to an old hardware store on rue du Bac, where she often purchases and takes home the French ceramic humidifier, a flat rectangle that holds water and is attached to apartment radiators. And her New York City windows are filled with Parisian metal plant holders in order to keep her geraniums sunning themselves halfway up her windows.

Why not begin at 63, rue de Grenelle, a very rarified *quartier* between Varenne and Bac? Walk to this address, where you will find one of seven locations of a very fine chain of pâtisseries. It's the

Dalloyau
63, rue de Grenelle, Paris 07
Telephone: 01.45.49.95.30
Metro: Bac
Closed: Saturday pm, Sundays

A top Parisian pâtisserie since 1802, with several shops in Paris and in Japan, Dalloyau is also a

chocolaterie, a *traiteur* (caterer), and a tea salon, with coffee and complete lunches as well as the best in pastries. (At a tea salon, you can always count on coffee with your excellent pastries.) It is one of the few places where, as in America, you can find everything together in one place. The Dalloyau that J. *et* G. know best is the one just across the street from the Luxembourg Gardens. At that salon, the pastries are all on the ground floor, and the tea room is upstairs.

Everything they serve—salads, smoked fish, smoked meats, and pastries—are of top quality and exquisite presentation. The *roulé marquis* (chocolate roll with raspberries) was Jeanette's choice for the day, with a splurge of two espressos to follow her pastry. Jeanette and Georgette have learned never to have a coffee with their dessert, but to do as the French do, and have that hit of strong, black caffeine following the scrumptious sweet.

Saving their taste buds for a less-known pastry from a different shop, J. *et* G. strolled down rue du Bac between Grenelle and Varenne, which has to be the very most chic stroll in Paris, with small boutiques of the finest clothing, stationery, haute coiffure, rugs and wallpapers, shoes, china, and jewelry. A short stroll, and a thrill to see where the French buy. Or at least the prosperous French.

Walking toward boulevard des Invalides on rue de Varenne, take a right toward the Seine on rue de Bourgogne until you come to one very elegant

Pâtissier-Traiteur-Chocolatier
Rollet Pradier
32, rue de Bourgogne, Paris 07
Telephone: 01.45.55.57.00
Metro: Assemblée Nationale,
Invalides
Closed: Mondays

There are more outstanding pastry shops in the 7th arrondissement than anywhere else in Paris. Our American readers know what competition does—you can be sure that they have to outdo each other to keep their profits. And as the French would say, you must *profiter de* (take advantage of) this competition in pastries when you go to the 7th arrondissement. When you go to see the Musée d'Orsay, you will want to wander around the streets of the 7th to experience a most authentic, upscale neighborhood of Paris.

Whenever you see *"traiteur,"* you are going to remember that J. *et* G. have already explained to you that a *traiteur* is a caterer. You can trust that the "take out" lunches, salads and pastries from Rollet Pradier are the Parisian best. Salads "to go" were exquisite: avocado and shrimp for €4.80,

aspic *au saumon* (salmon) for €3.65, and Georgette's favorite of the day, *salade niçoise* for €3.65. By now, you must know that J. *et* G. are going to say that it's much more fun to get a "take out" and eat it on the steps of the Orsay Museum to watch, hear, and taste the sweet life on the streets of Paris than to go to a nearby café. There is usually street music or pantomime, and once Jeanette and Georgette saw an enterprising student actor posing as the *Mona Lisa*! He was framed and struck such a resemblance that everyone contributed to his tin cup after they posed with him for this creative photo opportunity.

Chocolate lovers will have no choice—Rollet Pradier is the place to go. A "10" is an understatement for the chocolates you find in this shop! The pastry chef told J. *et* G. that they get many orders for chocolate birthday and saint's-day cakes. Children in France often celebrate both their birthday and their saint's day (every day of the year is a saint's day)—ask any French child the name of her birthday saint, and you'll see, she will be able to tell you! Besides chocolate, there are a few traditional, very expensive pastries, such as the *baba au rhum,* the *tarte aux framboises,* and the *opéra,* ranging up to €5. Jeanette looked and exuded while Georgette took notes, and both left happily without a purchase.

As the two stalkers of the sweet life walked toward the Place du Palais-Bourbon, they spotted a Caesar-like monument. On the monument was no name, no date, no nothing. Georgette knew that Jeannette would know what it was, because she knows all of the statues and sculptures of *gai Paree! Mais non,* Jeanette had no idea who this guy represented. Hunting around for clues, Georgette turned and spotted a very chic young French woman in a sports car that had slowed down as she got near the pâtisserie. G. rushed over to the car and asked, "What is that monument? Who is it? Why is it there?" *"Ben, alors,"* she replied. *"Ce n'est personne* [nobody]; it is only a Roman symbol of freedom and democracy," she said as she sped off in her own symbol of freedom.

Secco

20, rue Jean Nicot, Paris, 07
Telephone: 01.43.17.35.20
Metro: La Tour-Maubourg
Closed: Sundays and Mondays;
August

Jeanette and Georgette couldn't wait to get to Secco because they already knew what it looked like after seeing a picture in *Gourmet Magazine* of the Dalmatian painted below the front window, just sitting and waiting for his mistress to come out of the shop. This shop specializes in breads, and also *gâteau basque, pastis landais* (a brioche flavored with anise), and *cannelés de bordeaux.* There are nut- and fruit-flavored pound cakes, and fabulous-looking *mille-feuilles.* J. *et* G. could actually see hundreds of layers of the pastry in the *mille-feuilles,* and the pale-yellow custard-cream just oozed out of the sides. They had an iced rather than powdered-sugar topping, but Jeanette insists that some people prefer them that way. However, their eyes caught the *cannelé de bordeaux,* cylinder-shaped and two inches high, with a burnt outside and a soft, almond-flavored, moist cake inside. Excellent with coffee or tea, it is as close to bread and still cake as you can get. You will taste the wood-burning stove on the crust, which Georgette wasn't crazy about, but the Parisians seemed to be buying them as fast as they came out of the oven.

J. *et* G. found two pâtisseries off rue St-Dominique, on two tiny short streets: rue Jean Nicot and rue Surcouf. Jeanette quickly ran in to see the pastry shop on rue Surcouf, which is closed on Sundays and in August. But the traditional-looking pastries could hardly hold her attention because Georgette was so eager to get one of the seven tables at her favorite restaurant in the 7th. Just as Georgette looked down the street, she was surprised and tickled to see the owner-chef coming toward them on her way to work at

Au Petit Tonneau
Une cuisine de femme
20, rue Surcouf, Paris 07
Telephone: 01.47.05.09.01
Metro: La Tour-Maubourg
Closed: Never. Open every lunch
and dinner!

A character indeed, Ginette Boyer. Her chef's hat is taller than she is, perched on top of her ears above her oversized glasses. Originally from the Normandy region, she has created a small neighborhood restaurant (not far from the American Church of Paris— one of

two main Protestant churches, nondenominational, or at least it seems that way to Georgette). Ginette's cat and dog often can be seen running around the place. J. *et* G. got to know her because she loves to discuss issues with her customers, and she is as opinionated as Georgette. Georgette calls her "Madame Politique." You will think that you're watching a play in the dining room with the short, oldish chef yelling orders at the tall oldish waiter throughout the evening.

Ginette's specialties run according to the market, although Jeanette usually has her traditional *blanquette de veau,* or sometimes the steak or the *Normandie andouillette de Troyes dijonnaise,* a sausage in a frothy mustard-cream sauce, while Georgette loves to order the fresh coquille St-Jacques, which are almost always on the *plat du jour* menu. Even though you may hear and feel the typical French attitude toward Americans, *soyez courageux* (be brave). Go there anyway. You will find Au Petit Tonneau one of the few restaurants in the 7th with predominately French voices. It's truly a treat and you can expand Ginette's experience by verifying that Americans do indeed know world issues and good food and can take their time eating it.

After many years, Georgette finally got out of the chef her secret recipe for

Tarte Tatin
a.k.a. Tarte des Demoiselles Tatin

The Tatin sisters created this renowned dessert, but have never divulged their recipe. This famous country creation comes from their small French village hotel in Lamotte-Beuvron (about a hundred miles from Paris), which is still in operation. The Parisian version begins with spreading the butter thickly on the base of an iron pan. Sugar is poured over the butter. Apples are peeled, cored, halved, and arranged rounded-side-down. A puff pastry covers the apples. The pan is put over direct heat until the butter and sugar bubble and become a deep-amber color. Then the tart is baked in an oven until the puff pastry is cooked. It is then inverted as soon as it comes out of the oven, and served with the caramelized apples on top.

Jeanette told Georgette that not everyone cooks with general instructions, and some of our dear readers would want more specifics to bake their *tarte tatin*. Reluctantly, G. agreed to include measurements *exactement!*

First you make the flaky pastry dough:

1 cup flour
3 tablespoons softened sweet butter (the Parisians never use salted or
  even slightly salted butter)
3 tablespoons water
3 tablespoons cold butter

In a mixing bowl, place the flour and softened butter, broken into pieces. Mix with a pastry fork or by hand, and then add the salt and water. Form a ball with the dough. Place the dough in a second bowl and cover it with a plate. Let it stand for one hour in the refrigerator.

Rolling out the dough: place the cold butter between two sheets of waxed paper and tap it with the rolling pin to make it pliable. Lightly flour the dough and the rolling surface. Roll the dough out into a rectangle about 1/4-inch thick. Break the butter into pieces, and cover two-thirds of the dough with them. Fold the dough into thirds, beginning with the third which was not covered with butter. Turn the dough so that the line of the fold is perpendicular to you. Roll it out into a rectangle again; this time slightly less than 1/2-inch thick. Reflour the table and the dough whenever necessary, keeping it as lightly floured as possible. Fold the dough in fourths. Then fold the dough in half. Roll it out again less than 1/2-inch thick, and fold it in fourths again. Cover it well and chill it for one hour in the refrigerator. Roll out the dough 1/16-inch thick into a circle to fit your cast-iron baking dish. Place the dough on a plate and prick it with a fork. Refrigerate it while you prepare the apples:

2 3/4 pounds of tart cooking apples, peeled, cored, and halved
1/2 cup sweet butter
1 1/2 cup of granulated sugar

Preheat the over to 400°F. In a round cast-iron enameled dish, melt the butter and the sugar on top of the stove, and then place the apples very close together in the dish. Continue cooking very slowly until the sugar begins to caramelize. This should take at least 20 minutes and the apples should be soft. The caramel should be light brown.

Put the dish in the oven for 5 minutes, then cover the apples with the rolled-out flaky dough. Raise the oven temperature to 450°F and continue baking for 20 minutes or until the pie crust looks done. Once cooked, turn the dish over on a serving platter. Serve the tart warm. Resist the American temptation to add ice cream—be *très français* and add *crème fraîche* or, if you must, Georgette will agree to whipped cream.

Back to rue St-Dominique, where J. *et* G. came across the very elegant and romantic

Pâtisserie-Boulangerie Michel Arnoux
112, rue St-Dominique, Paris 07
Telephone: 01.45.51.31.01
Metro: La Tour-Maubourg
Closed: Sundays, Mondays

With marble floor, mosaic walls, chandeliers hanging from gilded ceiling, and an unusually bautiful wood-and-glass front, this traditional shop has four little burgundy tables where you can indulge in both pastry and coffee. If you are there to start the day, you will soon notice that everyone seems to be buying the specialty, *croissant aux amandes.* J. *et* G. looked at the *charlotte chocolate,* and the Normandy *tarte aux pommes* with hunks of apple and powdered sugar on top for €3. Georgette didn't like the *religieuse* because the cream was much too yellow and it had an unsavory-looking yellow icing trim that looked out of place in that elegant shop. But the fruit tarts looked luscious; the *tarte aux fraises* (strawberry) was Jeanette's choice. It had the best and most custard, and huge sweet berries, and was easy to divide in half at the little table. She wholeheartedly gave it a "9."

And close by they found

Boulangerie-Pâtisserie Putman Bertrand
145, rue Saint-Dominique, Paris, 07
Telephone: 01.45.51.43.86
Metro: La Tour-Maubourg
Closed: Sundays, Mondays

School's out! Teenagers packed the doorway of this beautiful pastry shop with the glass painting on the corner of the building. Parisian children get out of school on Wednesdays at noon, at which time they spend the afternoon in the park, or go to the cinema, or spend the time with their parents. This corner shop with a great window full of mouth-watering pastries stole the attention of most of the schoolchildren. Many young students stood at the window trying to persuade their parents to buy them a pastry. One ten-year-old boy said, "Je veux celle-là!" ("I want that one!")

"You won't eat it," replied the mother.

"Yes I will. I want that one."

"It's not worth the price," continued mama.

"Look, it's got fruit and sugar on top."

"But it's two euros!"

"Yes, it's only two euros . . . oh, *merci, maman!*"

After Jeanette and Georgette were well entertained by the school children, they gave a look to what was left. Something new! A *trois frères.* Too bad Georgette's brother John was not with them to share the "three brothers," three cream-filled pastry puffs—one vanilla, one coffee, and one chocolate. The *mille-feuilles* with powdered sugar were creamier than most, a jelly roll with raspberries on top looked wonderful, the *paris-brest* and the *bourdalouse* that the boy finally won did indeed look inviting. It was Georgette's turn, and she chose the *paris-brest.*

The shop is not far from St-Pierre du Gros Caillen (Petri A. Petra Magna), a small beautiful church—the perfect steps on which to eat a pastry from either of these shops. A perfect place to leave our beloved 7th arrondissement.

L'Histoire de Georgette et Ses Trois Pièces de Monnaie

The day began by setting out with determination to focus the day on Georgette's cashing in three coins (outmoded ten-franc pieces) from previous trips in the early 2000s. Every year she carried them to Paris and tried to cash them in at a different bank on the Champs-Elysées or the Place de l'Opéra, the two best places for highest rates for money exchange. Every year she was told, "Take them to the Bank of France. It's the only one that can cash your coins." Not having any idea where the bank was, J. *et* G.

Paris-Brest

This praline-flavored pastry was named for the famous Paris-to-Brest-to-Paris bicycle race. It builds from a round of *pâte à choux,* which is made from flour, eggs, water and butter. The puff pastry is split horizontally and the base is filled with pastry-custard mixed with whipped cream and praline paste folded in. Jeanette was told that praline paste was created by a French chef in 1598. It is a mixture of toasted almonds, hazelnuts, and caramelized sugar, one of the most delicious flavorings for custard creams and chocolates. The *paris-brest* is topped with another round of puff pastry and dusted with confectioner's sugar.

metroed to Palais Royal and looked for 39, rue Croix des Petits Champs. A guard told them that this door was not the entrance; they must walk to the other side.

Zut! Dear reader, wait until you see the length and width to the other side of the Bank of France! It must be three football fields long! (164 feet—well, almost two football fields long!) They rounded one corner, and then a second, and finally they went around a very long third corner until they exhaustedly found the entrance. Georgette spotted a huge, empty space with armed guards all around and one lonely little counter for commerce with three uniformed men sitting at it. An armed guard said to return the coins to the counter.

Georgette approached the first man, the one who looked the friendliest, and said *(en français, bien sûr)*: "I have three old ten-franc coins to exchange."

"*Non, trop tard* [too late]."

"What do you mean, '*trop tard*'? Here I am in the Bank of France, and this is *your* money, so please exchange it."

"*Non, non, non.* This has been out of circulation for five years. It's too late."

"How can it ever be too late? A Western European, hi-tech country like France doesn't even stand in back of its own currency?"

"*Non, trop tard.*"

"What can I do with it?"

"Give it to a museum."

"Jeanette, did you hear that? I'm leaving it right here on this counter!"

Very deflated, Georgette left the Bank of France with no new euros. How many pastries those three coins would have bought was her primary frustration.

They wandered across the street, and there, for the first time in their Paris travels, they came upon the spectacular Place des Victoires, a true paradox as they weren't feeling very victorious. But my, how the sights on Paris streets can lift the spirits—even when turned down by the Banque de France. Here are a circle of mansions built in the 1600s, with a statue of Louis XIV on a horse in the center of the square. Designers are now in those mansions: Kenzo, Cacharel, Esprit, and Thierry Mugler. This square reminded J. et G. somewhat of Place Vendôme, except it was smaller and the Place des Victoires was completely new to them. Looking around, they saw the tri-color French flag flying high and the beautiful clock face on top of the Bank of France, a wonderful sight even though Georgette had been foiled.

An earnest search began for the best pastry in the area, but not until Jeanette had reminded Georgette, after their walk around the Banque de France, that comfortable walking shoes must be emphasized in *Paris by Pastry*. Georgette said that wasn't necessary: All Americans wear comfortable walking shoes nowadays; Jeanette must be thinking back to earlier years in Paris, before running shoes were acceptable. With *pâtisseries* on their minds, they had only to cross rue Etienne Marcel, and voilà . . . joyously surprised, they discovered the most beautiful neighborhood pastry shop they had yet to see in Paris:

Au Panetier
10, place des Petits-Pères, Paris 02
Telephone: 01.42.60.90.23
Metro: Quatre Septembre, Palais-Royal
Closed: Sundays pm, Mondays

Tiles, chandeliers, ceilings were all magnificent. A steady stream of people—families, children, everyone—was buying and eating pastries on their way out, not even waiting for the unique Parisian wrapping. Jeanette *et* Georgette selected a *charlenoit.*

It was easy to find a place to eat the pastry. Just across the street from the pastry shop, but away from the Place des Victoires, J. *et* G. found the Basilique de Notre-Dame des Victoires. They went in for a look around and saw several people at prayer; no other onlookers were there at the time. Inside were 17th-century panels in the chancel, beautiful old oil paintings of St-Augustine's life, an 18th-century organ loft, and a monument to the 17th-century composer Jean-Baptiste Lully. Hushed and awed, J.

et G. came back out and sat quietly on the steps of the Basilique. Oh, what a church! Oh, what a city! *Quelle joie!* Georgette had finally forgotten about her lost coins.

Now for a taste of that *charlenoit* from that queen of pastry shops, Au Panetier.

Charlenoit

Just imagine hazelnut-almond meringue, smooth chocolate cream, and praline custard cream. A base of hazelnut-almond meringue, which is a consistency between a soft nut meringue and a sponge cake, is soaked with rum syrup. Spread with chocolate cream and another layer of cake and syrup, it is then layered with the praline custard cream, about one inch thick. After a third layer of cake is added and saturated with rum syrup, it is decorated on top with a large hazelnut surrounded with pale green marzipan leaves.

"Jeanette, did you bring the spoons?"

Félix Faure

Unless you were on a hunting expedition (for pastry and the delicious treat of capturing Parisian life and architecture in every nook and cranny of this magnificent city), there is no way you would end up on 32, avenue Félix Faure and the corner of rue Oscar Roty! If you take a chance (after all, Jeanette and Georgette aren't afraid of new places!), you will see that it's not too far to come to have a *soufflé aux fraises* (strawberry soufflé) for €3—like no other one in Paris!

Boulangerie-Pâtisserie
32, avenue Félix Faure, Paris 15
Telephone: 01.45.58.01.27
Metro: Boucicaut
Closed: Sundays pm, Mondays

At the corner of rue Oscar Roty, a short walk from the subway, they gave the *paris-brest,* fruit tarts, and *crème caramel* a "9+" on looks alone. Raymond *et* Marie-Thérèse Larsonneux are the patrons, and you'll find the pastries they serve you *elles valent la peine* ("well worth the pain"—or effort—as the French would say), to get there just to try their pastries.

Montparnasse

Always hunting the treasure of treasures—*la pièce de résistance*—Jeanette and Georgette set their sights near Montparnasse until they came up with Au Pain de Jean. Get off the metro at Vavin and cross the street to rue Delambre, in back of the famous Le Dôme restaurant. The Dôme is

Soufflé Chaud aux Fraises

This spectacular *soufflé* is prepared with a *crème pâtissière*, using egg yolks, milk, sugar, butter and flour. A sauce of strawberries is made by boiling fresh strawberries with a tablespoon of *eau de vie fraise* (strawberry brandy), sugar, and water, until it reaches the consistency of jam. The custard sauce and jam are mixed together and then beaten egg whites are folded in. The *soufflés* are assembled in individual soufflé dishes and baked for 10 minutes. Finally, they are dusted with icing sugar and served at room temperature. Sometimes, warm sauce is poured over the *soufflé* at the last minute. Jeanette tends to choose the fresh berries without the sauce, so she can take it outdoors to enjoy the sights and sounds of the Parisian streets as she eats her half of the delectable find.

famous for the freshest of fish and expensive prices. Its owner started Le Bistrot du Dôme on Delambre Street, right in back of his Dôme, and again, it offers the freshest of fish from the same fish market on Delambre, but at this restaurant for much less money. Do Jeanette and Georgette have to tell their readers that getting fresh fish and pastry next door to each other—at the right price—seems like heaven?

Au Pain de Jean
5, rue Delambre, Paris 14
Telephone: 01.43.35.41.54
Metro: Vavin
Closed: Mondays, Tuesdays;
August

Au Pain de Jean exhibited exotic tarts with kiwi and star fruit; ladyfingers in a row, filled with cream and apricots, looked uncommonly good. The *éclair* had a flat, rather than glossy, finish. Then there was an *éclair* cut like a hot dog roll and filled with coffee cream, with chocolate and powdered sugar on top. Very traditional pastries were all there, at reasonable prices. Don't miss this treasure on your pastry hunt— it should be among your tops.

Parc des Buttes-Chaumont

Husband: "Follow that path right there to the caves."

Wife: "No, don't send them that way!"

Husband: "That's the quickest way!"

Wife: "But it's not the prettiest way!"

Jeanette: "That's O.K." (All in French, *bien sûr.*) "We'll each take one way and meet at the caves."

Husband: "Oh *non!* Don't do that—those two paths never meet!"

So ended Jeanette's and Georgette's request for how to get to the caves in the Parc des Buttes-Chaumont: a very big, beautiful park with rocks, an island, caves, a Roman temple, a waterfall, footbridges leading to the island, beaches, and wilderness. J. *et* G. had taken the metro to Buttes-Chaumont and been absolutely charmed by this park. Walking across the footbridge, they kept going until they came out to the *mairie* (city hall) for the 19th arrondissement. On the inner circle, cross one street from the *mairie* to the pastry shop, directly

across the circle from the park fence. The most charming square, Place Armand Carrel, is where you will find the perfect pâtisserie:

Xavier Longueville
1, rue Meynadier, Paris 19
Telephone: 01.42.41.99.25
Metro: Laumière
Closed: Sundays, Mondays,
Wednesdays

A tea salon with six tables and wooden chairs. There were chocolate-covered *mille-feuilles,* and best of all, *oursin* (sea urchin) and *pomme de terre* (potato) look-alikes in pastry, with little sprouts coming out all over the potato, rolled in cocoa. All were reasonably priced at €1.50. But Jeanette and Georgette chose the raisin roll. It turns out that J. *et* G. didn't realize until they got home and read their notes that they hardly ever resisted the temptation to buy a raisin roll for their first-in-the-morning pastry! This one was ringed with warm, sweet custard, and baked with raisins and currants. J. *et* G. were in paradise . . . they had never tasted a better *pain aux raisins,* and they have had plenty to judge from!

Around the circle, there are benches on which to sit to eat your pastry and just watch the buses as they pull toward and away from the *mairie.* J. *et* G. were so enthralled by the area that they decided to go into the *mairie* to see what it looked like. It was quite like a small American city hall—police office on one side, people lined up waiting to go in for city business or a license of one kind or another—but then, in the center, a rotunda and glass peak, more Paris than New York.

Be sure to continue around the circle to Bistro Napoléon for your coffee at the *zinc* (Jeanette explained to Georgette that "zinc" is the French term for bar, because before World War II all the bar counters were covered in zinc. Georgette didn't ask but she assumed that Jeanette meant that they took the metal off all of the bars for the war effort.) The café has a green enamel front, a Dutch-looking woman running the bar, and Heineken on draft at their Dutch-tiled bar. The *plat du jour* was €8, and a baguette sandwich was €4. The tables look across the street to the park.

This delightful circle was indeed one of the top thrilling surprises of the trip. A small shop-lined street leads down to a different metro stop than J. et G. arrived on: Laumière. This section of Paris will remind you very much of a small French village outside of Paris. Of course if you aren't in the mood for a walk in the park, you can get to this unusual neighborhood within the Paris *périphérique* by starting at avenue Laumière and walking up the street to the Place Armand Carrel on rue du Rhin.

Place St-Georges

Georgette lived on rue Pigalle one summer when Jeanette was unable to go to Paris. Of course G. couldn't wait to introduce this *quartier* to J. when they returned. Starting at the metro St-Georges, there is a little triangle on which the Café St-Georges sits, and it is a perfect place for lunch, looking out on a small square with a monument of an actor *sans nom* (without a name!). This quaint, fascinating neighborhood is interspersed with antiques, art galleries, and theatres. The Parisians come here for two serious independent theatres, La Bruyère (5, rue La Bruyère) and the St-Georges (51, rue St-Georges), which are known for their risqué farce theatre. Georgette has to admit that this part of the treasure hunt is more for the theatre section, little-known by outsiders, than for the pastries. But wait! Walk north on rue Notre-Dame de Lorette from the Café St-Georges (except on a Monday, *n'oubliez pas*—don't forget), and on your left you will come to rue La Bruyère, where you will find

N. et H. Loge—Mumerel
35, rue La Bruyère, Paris 09

Telephone: 01.48.74.58.65
Metro: St-Georges
Closed: Sundays pm, Mondays; August

Jeanette and Georgette could not find anything good enough to buy right after a *salade niçoise* at the Café St-Georges, but if you are in the neighborhood to buy theatre tickets, choose the longest *éclairs* that J. *et* G. have ever yet seen in a pâtisserie.

If you want more from which to select your next treat, continue north on rue Notre-Dame de Lorette until you come to No. 64 at the corner of rue Pigalle, and there you will find a good pastry shop with everything at least a "7," although few "9s" and "10s." The view is the treasure! Look up to your right at this corner and see the Sacré-Coeur hovering like a mirage above you; look straight ahead and you will see the old windmill of the Moulin Rouge, the Montmartre can-can night club where Henri de Toulouse-Lautrec sketched his posters.

Now. Take a left and walk south down (south) rue Pigalle for four blocks (passing a superb, traditional restaurant, Le Bistro des Deux Théâtres, at 18, rue Blanche, telephone 01.45.26.41.43), and you will come to Square de la Trinité. At the square, you will find a beautiful gothic church, Trinité, which is not noted in any Paris

guides except *Paris by Pastry!* When J. *et* G. went in, they listened to a lovely soprano voice rehearsing at the organ, which provided wonderful background music as they studied the candelabra and brass chandeliers, the gold altar, marble columns, and powder-blue star-studded ceiling. The ceiling reminded Georgette of the one at Grand Central Station where she always meets Jeanette in New York City. There is a metro right at Trinité, to catch for your next delight. Theatre students and lovers of authentic cafés, don't miss the St-Georges treasures!

Expédition de Françoise

It is in the home of Françoise that Georgette and Jeanette have made their *résidence française* as often as they could be in Paris during the past decade. Originally from Bordeaux, Françoise has lived in Paris for the past thirty years, in the home of her grandfather. Even though she appeared quite cool about their pastry project, one day in July as she was leaving for a mountain trek, Françoise admitted to Georgette that she had mentioned the *Paris by Pastry* idea to her companion, and much to her surprise learned that although he had moved to another *quartier* (neighborhood) recently, he continued to return to his old

neighborhood for his pastries. Of course Françoise has a favorite pâtisserie (**Vaudron**) in her neighborhood, as the Parisians do, but she really wasn't aware that her friends had the same loyal regard for their neighborhood pastry haunts. When she started asking around, Françoise learned that some of her friends even traveled way across the city to buy from the shop that they adored. J. *et* G. were eager to know what a Parisian's favorite pastry shops are, so Françoise agreed to query her friends and to share with Jeanette and Georgette their top half-dozen. In order of priority, then, follow Françoise around Paris and hunt the rarified species of Parisians' most-wanted pâtisseries according to

Françoise's Top Half-Dozen Pâtisseries

1. **Vaudron,** 4, rue de la Jonquière, Paris 17; Metro: Guy-Moquet; Telephone: 01.46.27.96.97; Closed: Mondays. (See above.)
2. **Dalloyau,** 101, rue du Faubourg-Saint-Honoré, Paris 08; Metro: St-Philippe-du-Roule; Telephone: 01.42.99.90. 00; Closed: Never. (See pages 12, 31)
3. **Lenôtre,** 15, blvd de Courcelles, Paris 08; Metro: Villiers; Telephone: 01.45.63.87.63; Closed: Never. (Gaston Lenôtre is a master pastry chef with students and shops all over Paris and France.)
4. **Ladurée,** 21, rue Bonaparte, Paris 06; Metro: St-Germain-des-Prés; Telephone: 01.44.07.64.87; Closed: Sundays. August. (See pages 59, 123.)
5. **Le Triomphe,** 23, rue du Rendez-vous, Paris 12; Metro: Place de la Nation; Telephone: 01.20.02.08.79; Closed: Sunday PM, Mondays. (See page 97.)
6. **Boulangerie Aurélie et Franck Veau,** Square St-Cyr, 55 blvd Gouvion, Paris 17; Metro: Porte Maillot; Telephone: 01.45.74.04.50; Closed: Wednesdays. (See page 51.)

Vaudron began its pastry business in 1931 and has been consistently excellent ever since. It is the best-rated pâtisserie (according to J. *et* G., who know best) that is closest to where Françoise lives; it has become the favorite of J. *et* G. because they have never had a disappointing taste or smell or texture or look, and never tasted a pastry below a "9" in twenty years of hunting the delicious in Paris. It is from Françoise that Jeanette and Georgette learned that in France, a macaroon—the only pastry that she ever asked them to bring home for her—is not made of coconut! They gave this truly French favorite a try.

Macarons (Macaroons)

There is no coconut in French macaroons. They are the most delicate petits fours: light, soft, shiny and smooth on the outside, and best of all, chewy in the center. The meringue-and-ground-almonds cookie—vanilla, *fraise* (strawberry), chocolate, or coffee—is made from egg whites and sugar, and filled sometimes with red currant jelly but usually with a flavored buttercream frosting. Georgette doesn't even like coffee pastries, and yet has to admit that she found a coffee macaroon absolutely out of this world! Here is the extra-delicate, fine-textured coffee macaroon recipe, straight from the chef of Vaudron!

But wait . . . How many of our dear readers know where to buy almond paste? Raise your hands! Keep your hands up . . . Now, how many of you know how to make it at home? That's what Jeanette *et* Georgette were afraid of. So before we begin, here is the recipe that you will need for one batch (100 halves to make 50) of coffee macaroons. But first— 9 ounces of

Homemade Almond Paste
3/4 cup powdered almonds
A scant (5/6) cup confectioner's sugar
1 egg white from a small egg

Mix the almond powder with the sugar, then add the egg white and blend until smooth. Now we are ready for

Coffee Macaroons
9 ounces almond paste (recipe above or store-bought)
7 egg whites, large
1 teaspoon coffee extract
1³/4 cups sugar

Line two large baking sheets with baking parchment. Fit pastry bag with a plain round 1/2-inch tip.

Beat or knead almond paste with 1 egg white and the coffee extract. Set aside. In bowl of electric mixer, whip egg whites until soft peaks form, then add sugar. Beat at medium-high speed until very stiff and glossy. Blend in the almond paste. Transfer to pastry bag and pipe out 1-inch mounds on the prepared baking sheets. Let dry for 3 hours so that macaroons form a light crust. This prevents them from collapsing in the oven.

Preheat oven to 275°F. Bake macaroons for 25 minutes, until lightly colored and crisp. Allow to cool on the parchment paper. Turn the macaroons over, parchment paper and all, and moisten the reverse side of the paper with a damp cloth. In a few minutes the macaroons will easily come away from the baking parchment. Make a coffee- or chocolate-flavored *crème au beurre* to add a sweet filling that will stick together the flat sides of the macaroons. Oh no! You don't know how to make a coffee-flavored *crème au beurre* filling?? *C'est la vie* . . . Here it is:

Crème au Beurre au Café

1 stick (1/2 cup) sweet butter
1/3 cup sugar
1 tablespoon water
1 egg
11/4 teaspoons of coffee extract (do not use instant coffee)

Cut the butter into small chunks and set aside. In a small saucepan, cook the sugar and water over low heat to the soft ball stage (242°F on a candy thermometer). Beat the egg at high speed in a deep mixing bowl until light and fluffy. When the sugar is ready, pour it over the egg, between the side of the bowl and the beaters, beating all the time to avoid cooking the eggs. Beat for another 10 minutes, until almost cool, then beat in the butter, two or three chunks at a time. The frosting will suddenly thicken as you add the last third of the butter. Add 1 teaspoon of coffee extract and continue beating until perfectly smooth and creamy. Keep at room temperature until you are ready to put a thin layer on the flat surface of two of the macaroons.

Voilà! You will be invited to every tea party in the neighborhood when you promise to bring a batch of your famous coffee macaroons. Georgette thinks they also go well with champagne. Try it!

Paris Prizes
More Top Attractions

Some would say that the Arc de Triomphe, the Centre Pompidou, and the Place des Vosges are attractions that you wouldn't think of missing on your first trip to Paris. So if you have three days in Paris and you want to include the highlights, then make your way to Montmartre, the Place de l'Opéra, La Madeleine, and Parc Monceau to take it all in. Just wait until you are the one envied as you sit on the park bench or museum and church steps with a Parisian pastry in hand as you enjoy the aesthetic as well as the sweet treats not to be matched

anywhere in the world.

Arc de Triomphe
Place Charles de Gaulle
Metro: Charles de Gaulle-Etoile

Françoise, Jeanette's and Georgette's Parisian friend, began to get involved with the *Paris by Pastry* research because they brought a different pastry home each evening for a tasting (to share three ways, *bien sûr*). Here is a shop that Françoise recommended, because her trekking companion drove out of his way every day except Wednesday to get his favorite pastry taste.

Boulangerie Aurélie et Franck Veau
Square St-Cyr, 55, blvd Gouvion, Paris 17
Telephone: 01.45.74.04.50
Metro: Porte Maillot
Closed: Wednesdays

It was Bastille Day! July 14th— Jeanette and Georgette wanted to head toward the Arc de Triomphe to see the annual parade. They had heard that the German army was going to march down the Champs-Elysées for the first time since General Charles de Gaulle led his soldiers in a parade from the Arc to Notre-Dame Cathedral for a victory Mass on August 26, 1944. J. *et* G. took the metro to Charles de Gaulle, at the Arc, and then walked up the avenue of the Grand Army toward Porte Maillot until they came to boulevard Gouvion and found the pastry shop. They saw soldiers and tanks from all of Western Europe, moving in all directions to get in line to go through the Arc de Triomphe. They hurried along, lured by the exuberance of the French celebration, with Françoise's hand-drawn map in hand, but alas, without the street address of the pastry shop in question. In the excitement of the day, they still didn't get the address.

Lucky for our dear readers, J. *et*

G. stalked until they found a lovely residential neighborhood with magnificent apartment buildings. The Boulangerie Aurélie et Franck Veau is located on a little triangle. *Les gâteaux* (cakes) appeared to be their specialty, mostly cakes with cream and fresh fruit. There were refrigerated glass showcases displaying the cakes, but the pastry that got Jeanette's attention was the *tulipe chantilly*, a boat-shaped pastry with scalloped edges filled with cream and strawberries. Also featured in the shop was a fantastic-looking *crème brûlée*, and a specialty of apple cakes with calvados (liqueur made from apple cider). And nuts: many walnut desserts and a *sablé* (shortbread) covered with chocolate and walnuts. An unusual array of *gâteaux*—small wonder that Françoise's friend made sure to get to this shop every day! A bench right outside the shop was perfect to sit on and eat the *tulipe* while taking in the magnificent 19th-century apartment buildings in the area.

J. *et* G. walked across the street, where a wonderful window display drew them into the shop of

Au Petit Duc
48, boulevard Gouvion St-Cyr, Paris 17
Metro: Porte Maillot
Telephone: 01.45.74.85.51
Closed: Mondays; no annual closure

An upscale pâtisserie and *chocolaterie*—just what you would expect in this swanky neighborhood. There were cakes and tarts and many cream pastries with fresh pears to boot! Jeanette was captivated by a real American-looking chocolate pudding with a raspberry on top. Needing a pastry to go, it was hard to choose between the *chiboust aux poires* (pastry cream and pear in a pastry shell), a *gâteau* of blue, white, and red (the traditional Bastille Day pastry), or the *framboise-champagne*. Given the celebratory occasion of the 14th of July, they decided to go with the champagne. The pastry was filled with a champagne cream custard and presented with swirls and peaks, it had fresh wild raspberries folded into the light cream, and it was topped with fresh berries. The *framboise-champagne* was fastidiously wrapped in a neat little box, an unusual packaging for a pâtisserie, but common for those who specialize in creams.

As the pastry was being wrapped, Jeanette and Georgette heard a very loud rumbling sound, which came closer and closer until they realized it must be one of those tanks heading for the Arc de Triomphe. They both rushed out the door, and there, riding atop the tank, were French soldiers, the French blue, white, and red flag flying high, going at great speed in a big noise. Georgette ran back into the shop to grab their pastry, and both started to run in the direction of the Arc de Triomphe. As they got closer to the Arc, they could see an enormous French flag hanging from inside. They quickly found a sidewalk café where they sipped their coffee and watched the parade. It was while standing there with their coffee that they witnessed the rumbling tanks followed by marching soldiers. Then they spotted the German military coming up to and through the Arc de Triomphe. Goose pimples covered Georgette's skin, as she thought, "If I feel emotional over the first march of German soldiers down the Champs-Elysées since World War II, how on earth do the French bear it?" J. *et* G. agreed it was a generous spirit of diplomacy on the part of the French, and the future is indeed symbolized by hope. With that thought, they went to visit the Tomb of the Unknown Soldier, which commemorates the dead soldiers of World War I. They solemnly got back on the metro at Charles de Gaulle and went quietly and pensively home.

Montmartre

When Jeanette and Georgette began to spend their summers in Paris, they first rented an apartment—sight unseen—from a young American who had gone to Paris instead of to college. She had then returned to the U.S. with her newfound French boyfriend to attend summer school. J. *et* G. soon learned the French ways in this 18th-arrondissement neighborhood on rue Doudeauville. The closest pastry shop—for their daily bread and pastry—was closed on Sunday mornings, so every Sunday morning they crossed boulevard Barbès and started up rue Custine toward Montmartre because they had found a wonderful pâtisserie that had the very best butter croissants and *pains aux raisins* (raisin rolls). But the shop's specialty, which remained true ten years later when they were researching *Paris by Pastry*, was the *chausson aux pommes.* As Georgette sits in Vermont on a Sunday morning, she can just picture that walk up Custine, smell that pastry shop, see those pastries, and taste that crispy, flaky crust as she bites down into the warm apple filling . . . Oh, to start the week in *la belle ville de Paris* every Sunday morning! Even though J. *et* G. were tempted by the *tarte exotique* with kiwi fruit, it was the *chausson aux pommes* that won their €1.80 and grade of "9+." Carefully testing the taste, texture, and aroma, *mais oui*, they found the morning breads were just as good as their high expectations. *Ohhh là là!* If you want a different path to Montmartre, climbing up through a residential neighborhood, take the metro to Château Rouge, pick up a

pastry at 16, rue Custine, and continue your climb up the stairs to Monmartre—the crown of Paris. Jeanette told Georgette to be sure to tell our dear readers that the Château Rouge *quartier* has gone downhill so much, that not even to save money would J. *et* G. live there these days.

In all the years Jeanette and Georgette have stayed in Paris, they had never taken the funicular to Montmartre. Jeanette wants her readers to know that they can use their regular metro ticket (but of course she expects *Paris by Pastry* readers to have bought a *carte orange* by now) for this ride. True, they lived within walking distance, going another way to the top; still, you'd think that Jeanette with all her French student trips would have taken it at least once! For the first time, they took the metro to Anvers, walked two blocks to the Place St-Pierre, and then started looking for pastries along the route. Yuk! No wonder they had never gone this way—it was loaded with junk, fabrics, and souvenirs all along rue de Steinkerque, the main street leading to the funicular. There were several cafeterias, self-serve restaurants with fruit tarts and flans too ordinary to pay for or eat. If you can't wait, however, until you get to the top, or if there is a long line and wait at the funicular, on 1, rue Tardieu, right opposite the funicular, you will find

Le Gastelier

1, rue Tardieu, Paris 18
Telephone: 01.46.06.22.06
Metro: Anvers
Open: every day in summer
Closed: Mondays in winter

There are *éclairs* for €1.50, *religieuses* for €2, *mille-feuilles*, *cherubin* (cheesecake) *aux fraises* or *framboises,* and even tiramisu for €3. Everything looked at least a "5 +," and for the honky-tonk neighborhood—*pas mal* (not bad)!

Jeanette *et* Georgette do not eat "5" pastries, however, so, 427 feet up on top (the highest point in Paris) J. *et* G. found the thrilling excitement of an artist-writer village with all the hustle of the portrait artists in the Place du Tertre (where Jeanette threatens to have a portrait sketched someday of Georgette eating a succulent pastry), the Edith Piaf–like singers wandering the narrow crooked streets, marionette shows, abundant crafts and jewelry, and sidewalk bistros loaded with tourists having coffee or beer at La Mère Catherine, the pink bistro on the square that is probably the most painted and photographed bistro in Paris. Topping it all off is the Roman-Byzantine church, the Sacré-Coeur, seen from all over Paris as if it were a white marble cathedral in the sky.

The only excellent pastry shop is

La Galette des Moulins

1 Terrace, rue Norvins, Paris 18,
at Place Jean-Baptiste Clément
Telephone: 01.42.64.17.00
Metro: Anvers
Closed: Sundays, Mondays

Once up on Montmartre, a top tourist attraction of Paris, J. *et* G. found this the one pâtisserie worth considering—with everything at least a "7" or "8." This shop also had sandwiches and wonderful-looking petit macaroons, but they tried the *concorde* for €3 and were not disappointed.

Sitting on the curb at the high north end, looking out over all of Paris, is worth the crowd and the many souvenir shops of Montmartre. J. *et* G. shared their pastry, pointed out to each other in the distance Notre-Dame, the Galeries Lafayette, the Louvre, and the Panthéon, and dreamed of their return.

Centre Pompidou

Rue du Renard, Paris 04
Telephone: 01.44.78.12.33
Metro: Hôtel de Ville, Châtelet,
Les Halles
Bus: 38, 47, 69, 72, 74, 76, 85
Closed: Tuesdays; May 1

If you want sweet music, modern art, people-action, students gathering, and hanging out, you will find it all in the Les Halles area, the old "belly of Paris," as Emile Zola described it back in the 19th century. Head for the square outside the Pompidou Center. If the few hippies left in the world from Eugene, Oregon, Olympia, Washington, and Santa Cruz, California, find themselves in Europe beyond Amsterdam, they will be here. South and Central American music is prevalent along with all kinds of street entertainment. Finding the best and closest pastry to eat while sitting on a stone pillar—seat height, while you bask in the sun admiring the "inside out" rib cage of this modern architecture—is your task at hand. It's so much like a circus around here, with all the fast foods (Bagelry, Food Time, and McDonald's), Les Halles bargains, outdoor racks of clothes, and the underground cinema, swimming pool, and restaurants, that you may be as surprisingly shocked as Jeanette and Georgette were to find the most elegant pâtisserie three doors down from the front of the Pompidou Center.

Boulangerie-Pâtisserie
D. Béatrix
149, rue St-Martin, Paris 03
Telephone: 01.42.72.64.60
Metro: Châtelet, Les Halles, Hôtel-de-Ville
Closed: Mondays

Not only will you discover the most

Concorde

A chocolate meringue is baked in an oval shape made of spirals squeezed out of the pastry bag. Once this is done, the rest of the meringue is baked in long strips. After it cools, a layer of chocolate mousse is spread over the meringue. A second oval layer of chocolate meringue is placed over the mousse, then a second layer of mousse, and finally the last layer of meringue. The cake is completely covered with the remaining mousse. The chocolate meringue strips are cut into sticks and used to cover the sides and top. The cake is sprinkled all over with powdered sugar and cut into wedges. Chocolate lovers? Try the *concorde*!

elegant pastries, but there is also a tiny coffee bar with a few stools at the end of the shop, and out front three of the tiniest tables that you are likely to find. The shop appears to be all glass—a showcase in a

narrow passageway to walk along while you ponder your selection. A group of university students from Madrid were looking over the pastries as Georgette looked at the pear tarts (€2.30) and *sablés* (cookies), and then selected a *divorcée*. Can you imagine what a *divorcée* is? It's a cream puff divided into chocolate on one side and coffee on the other, each with its own territory (flavor) and icing of the same. One could also call it "to each one's own." We have to assume that the French think that compromise is the answer to a good marriage, and that the married couple should be able to choose either chocolate or coffee! Or we could assume, by the name of this pastry, that divorce is the result of the inability to give in to the chocolate or coffee happiness of the other. Georgette chose the *divorcée* because Jeanette loves coffee and Georgette doesn't, while Jeanette saved their two seats (stone pillars). Georgette ran back to tell Jeanette the big news of the moment: a most wonderful pastry shop can be found very near the Pompidou Center—at 149, rue Saint-Martin.

In another direction from the Pompidou, you can't miss the magnificent Eglise St-Merri. While looking all around, J. *et* G. met a character who hangs out around there who explained (*en français, bien sûr!*) that the St-Merri area was historically the home of the first craftsmen in Paris. In the Middle Ages there were lacemakers and linendrapers in this neighborhood, and according to him, Parisian fashions began right here. He went on to say that it was in the St-Merri Quarter that a young boy and an old man were killed in 1832, the event upon which Victor Hugo based *Les Misérables*. Pastry in hand, the pastry-hunters staggered away with their heads much more full of fascinating facts than were their hands and thoughts of pastries.

Whenever you've had it with the crowds at the Pompidou Center, take your best pastry and head for the shade and a fountain. Walk three blocks to the Square of

Innocents at the corner of rue Aubry le Boucher (which turns into rue Berger) and rue St-Denis. The glorious fountain here was moved to the Les Halles area in the 18th century; it is the only Renaissance fountain left in Paris. Students are attracted to fountains in Paris, and this is one place where they can count on finding one. Speaking of fountains, if you have studied the *French in Action* program in high school or college, or seen it on PBS, you will recognize the Pompidou Center pool with the big-red-lips fountain that closes each video lesson. If you want more shade than fountain, keep walking on rue Berger to find the Forum des Halles which is surrounded by a park. When you come to rue Berger and rue Supervielle, you will find a planting of very beautiful trees, and also some benches just a short hike away. (Jeanette says that "hike" is the key word here.) Even with thousands of people walking about, the distances are vast, so conserve your energy and remember: good pastries are very scarce in this area.

Georgette likes her pastries on church steps best, and she found two: Eglise St-Merri, known for its design and woodwork from the 14th century, with the oldest church bell in Paris, dating from 1331. Or the Gothic St-Eustache, one of the most beautiful churches in Paris, modeled after Notre-Dame and completed in 1637. Molière, the great 17th-century playwright, was baptized here. The French love to mix the old with the new. The modern sculpture of a hand and Buddha-like head in front of the Gothic St-Eustache is a wonderful example of this. The sculpture is for touching—children are all over it.

Before you leave the Modern Art Pompidou Center, you will surely want to check out the portrait of the journalist Sylvia von Harden by Otto Dix, *Le magasin de Ben* ("Ben's Store") by Benjamin Vautier, and of course the masterpieces of Matisse, Miró, Picasso, Braque, Calder, and the all-American Pollock. Riding up the outdoor escalator will keep children entertained for more than their usual attention span at museums. The view from the top is impressive even to Françoise, J. *et* G.'s Parisian friend who first took them there. If it's lunch time after your tour of the Pompidou Center, make your way to the back of the building on rue du Renard to the Excelsior for lunch or a coffee at the table or at the bar. Given the honky-tonk flavor of the area, and not wanting a circus lunch, you will love this authentic Parisian brasserie.

Madeleine

Place de la Madeleine, Paris 08
Telephone: 01.42.65.52.17
Metro: Madeleine, Concorde
Closed: 7 pm

Of course you can't miss this magnificent early 17th-century Greek-like temple. Madeleine's immense fifty-two Corinthian columns rise to glory with lavishly decorated marble, gilt, and a sculpture of *Mary Magdalene Ascending to Heaven* in back of the high altar. Still, the Place de la Madeleine is probably known best by pastry- and food-lovers for Fauchon, the millionaire's gourmet mall! And well known, too, for its open-air flower market.

J. *et* G. know that the little lemon tea cakes baked in a scallop-shell mold, *madeleines*, are one of the best-known and easiest-to-bake Parisian *pâtisseries*. Jeanette insists on a recipe so that we can mention Marcel Proust, who, J. tells G., once dipped a *madeleine* into his tea, only to have all his memories come flooding back. A philosopher at heart, she does the same! Here is your road back to childhood memories:

Madeleines

1 stick softened sweet butter
2/3 cup sugar
3 eggs
Rind of 1 lemon, finely-grated
2/3 cup flour
1/4 teaspoon salt
1/4 teaspoon baking powder

Preheat oven to 350°F. In a large mixing bowl, cream butter and sugar until light. Beat in whole eggs, then lemon rind. Place the mixture over a pot of hot water and beat until creamy. In a small bowl, mix together dry ingredients, and then beat into butter mixture until well blended. Fill silicone madeleine molds to about half-full, and bake 10 to 12 minutes until golden brown. Serve warm, dip into tea, and sweet memories will rise from the senses . . .

Before going to the Place de la Madeleine, Jeanette and Georgette always like to get off the metro at the Concorde exit and walk up rue Royale toward the exquisite south bronze door portraying the Ten Commandments. *Naturellement*, they can't resist stopping first, for their pastry to be eaten in La Place de la Madeleine, at

Ladurée
16, rue Royale, Paris 08
Telephone: 01.42.60.21.79
Metro: Concorde, Madeleine
Closed: Sundays; August

A *très, très* elegant tea salon and pâtisserie, Ladurée has all of the fruit tarts, puff pastries, and cakes that you will ever dream of tasting. If it's cold or rainy and you don't feel like eating on the glorious steps of Madeleine, you can sit at a small table right here and, without budging, have an after-pastry coffee as well. Even though they had never heard of a *cramique*, and it looked too good to resist, Jeanette and Georgette did turn down this raisin-filled brioche. Instead, J. *et* G. were eager to try the *gâteaux* (cakes)— expensive, but the best—and chose *la truffe: sauce anglaise au café* (chocolate truffle cake with coffee custard). Sitting on the steps in front of the gigantic representation of the *Last Judgment* on the south side of

Madeleine, they dipped their spoons into a chocolate-sponge base brushed with cognac, layered with a mixture of whipped cream and melted bitter chocolate, and sprinkled with cocoa on top. They had persuaded Mademoiselle to put the sauce in a separate little cup, so that they could add the coffee-flavored *crème anglaise* at the moment of truth (seated in the perfect Parisian setting and ready to savor another pastry).

Now, everyone knows that it's always better to go to a food store on a full stomach, otherwise, you end up buying everything in sight. So, walk around to the north side of Madeleine, to 26, Place de la Madeleine. Take the time to study the aesthetic window presentation of the food from all over the world. To get a sense of the wealth of offerings of the more than 20,000 products sold at Fauchon, just head for the mustard section: a whole room with shelves packed with every kind of mustard imaginable . . . and then some! A Parisian experience to treasure. Once J. *et* G. went to Fauchon at lunch time, and sampled a forkful of this and a forkful of that at the salad and fish "stand-up" self-service cafeteria. Since then, Fauchon has added a café where you can sit and lunch, but needless to say, it's difficult to get as many tastes as when you help yourself! Such indulgence will enhance your culinary *savoir-faire* (know-how).

With pastries in mind, you must know, *cher lecteur* (dear reader), that it has to look awfully good after that rich truffle, and it did! J. *et* G. chose to take home for dinner the raspberry *vacherin*. You have to see it to believe it. The base is made with a French meringue (egg whites and sugar), the center is a tart raspberry gelatin, the top is a layer of chantilly cream (vanilla-flavored whipped cream) literally covering the top and sides of the raspberry center. The sides are decorated with ovals of meringue pressed against the cream. The space in the center is filled with fresh raspberries, with a touch of sauce spooned over the top. Ah, *oui*, won't Françoise be thrilled with today's find?

Place de l'Opéra

Place de l'Opéra, Paris 09
Telephone: 01.47.42.57.50
Metro: Opéra
Closed: Holidays

The opera is no longer presented in this majestic, Second Empire opulent structure; however you must not miss this "old" opera house! If the ballet is performing there while you are in Paris, do go, whether you like ballet or not. Finding your seat by way of the white-marble grand foyer and staircase for a performance will be reward enough. Inside you will see the six-ton chandelier and tiers of red velvet and gold, all topped with a ceiling of Marc Chagall's masterpiece depicting Parisian opera images. Tours are given daily, or you could just go and stand in the foyer and see the staircase without spending your euros. Jeanette and Georgette never spend money to see what they can see without spending it. They never take a tour if they can go to a performance in a church, a cathedral or the Opéra de Paris! Even if they aren't crazy about the performance, there is something to be said for authentic attendance. Observation of the French in particular settings increases your understanding of the French. J. *et* G. always go to the Place de l'Opéra by way of the metro, so that they can walk out the Opéra exit, never turning around until they are at the top of the steps leading out, directly across from the entrance, when they turn in unison and *voilà*! The thrill of seeing Apollo lifting his lyre above his head, of spotting the busts of famous composers, of viewing winged horses and eyeing ornate within ornate. This is *gai* Paree! It's the one tourist area where Georgette agrees to sit for a coffee at the Café de la Paix, providing it isn't

July or August, just to gaze at the columns, friezes, and sculptures of the old Paris Opera.

Leave the Place de l'Opéra and walk down rue de la Paix toward the elegant shopping of Place Vendôme, where the Ritz is located and where Jeanette used to make her annual visits to the former Michel Swiss, the discount, duty-free shop of her choice. She bought perfume, cosmetics, soap, designer ties, and sometimes a piece of jewelry to take back to her relatives and friends. Nowadays, Americans buy these Parisian specialties in the airports' duty-free shops instead of on Paris's magnificent rue de la Paix!

Concerning their pastry-research task of the day, there is no question that Jeanette and Georgette tried. They searched, hunted, and stalked the area around the Place de l'Opéra and the Café de la Paix for a single pastry shop. They walked from the Opéra metro station to the boulevard des Italiens on the east, from l'Opéra to La Madeleine on the west, from l'Opéra to rue Chaussée-d'Antin on the north, from l'Opéra to la Place des Pyramides on the south. They even came back another time, not trusting that the first hunt was thorough enough for their dear readers. The only advice to be offered when visiting the Place de l'Opéra—is to take your pastry with you from rue St-Honoré (p.7), or from the Boulangerie de la Fontaine Gallion, the stockbrokers' pastry shop (p.115). For this one time, if you can't go another minute without a French pastry—you crave a seat, a coffee, and a hit of sweet—then you have the permission, in this case alone, of J. *et* G. to spend the money and order a pastry from the Café de la Paix. We admit that it's hard to believe that there are no pastry shops near the place de l'Opéra. If Jeanette *et* Georgette say so . . . believe it!

Georgette was so disappointed not to find a perfect *pâtisserie* to remind her of the Place de l'Opéra that she went right home (G. now calls the home of Françoise "her" home), looked up the recipe for the *pâtisserie* named in its honor. In order for her dear readers to have a taste of this chocolate-glazed cake with coffee buttercream, she is going to let them in on this rich and elegant layered pastry that matches that of the architectural masterpiece of Charles Garnier. Before you begin, though, Georgette wants to be sure that her readers know, it ain't easy!

Gâteau Opéra

1 10x5-inch *biscuit joconde* (almond sponge cake)
1/2 cup *sirop à entremets* (dessert syrup) *à la vanille* or *au Grand Marnier*
1 cup *crème au beurre au café* (coffee buttercream)
1/3 cup *ganache à la vanille* (chocolate cream vanilla frosting)
5/8 cup *glaçage au chocolat* (chocolate glaze)

Starting with the sponge-cake part, here is

Biscuit Joconde
2/3 cup ground blanched almonds
1/3 cup sugar
2 eggs
3 tablespoons flour
3 egg whites, pinch of salt
1 tablespoon sugar
2 tablespoons sweet butter, melted

Preheat oven to 350°F. Butter a 10x15-inch jellyroll pan and line with waxed paper. Butter the paper. In a large mixing bowl, stir together almonds and sugar, then whisk in whole eggs and beat until smooth. Add flour and beat just until well blended.

In a deep mixing bowl, beat egg whites and salt at high speed until soft peaks form. Add sugar and continue beating until stiff but not dry. Beat one-third of whites into batter, and then carefully fold in rest of whites. Finally, fold in butter.

With a rubber spatula, spread batter evenly over baking sheet. Bake 8 to 10 minutes, until biscuit is light brown around the edges and cream-colored in the middle. Remove from oven, invert onto a sheet of waxed paper, and brush hot waxed paper on bottom with cold water. Wait a few minutes, and then carefully peel off waxed paper.

Next comes the preparation for

Grand Marnier Syrup
1/4 cup sugar
1/4 cup water
1 tablespoon of Grand Marnier

In a saucepan, heat sugar and water to a boil. Cool, then stir in Grand Marnier (or vanilla if you don't want to spend your money on a bottle of Grand Marnier just for this recipe!).

And now it's on to the

Crème au Beurre au Café
1 stick (1/2 cup) sweet butter
1/3 cup sugar
1 tablespoon water
1 egg
1+ teaspoon coffee extract

Cut the butter into small chunks and set aside. In a small saucepan, cook the sugar and water over low heat to the soft ball stage (242°F on a candy thermometer).

While the sugar cools, beat the egg at high speed in a deep mixing bowl until light and fluffy. When the sugar is ready, pour it over the egg, between the side of the bowl and the beaters, beating constantly.

Beat for 10 minutes, until almost cool, then beat in the butter 2 or 3 chunks at a time. The frosting, liquid at first, will suddenly thicken as you add the last third of the butter. Continue beating until perfectly smooth and creamy. Beat in a heaping teaspoon of coffee extract. (Can you heap a teaspoon of liquid? *Je crois que non!* Georgette means a teaspoon plus a little more).

Almost done! Here's the

Ganache à la Vanille
2¹/₂ ounces semi-sweet chocolate
3 tablespoons of heavy cream
¹/₂ teaspoon vanilla extract

In a double boiler, heat chocolate and cream until chocolate is completely melted. With a wooden spoon, stir until smooth, then stir in vanilla. Cool thoroughly before using. *Ganâche* should be very thick, but if it's too thick to spread, stir in a few more drops of heavy cream until you can spread it.
Ensuite . . . (And then . . .)

Glaçage au Chocolat
4 ounces semi-sweet chocolate
¹/₂ tablespoon sweet butter
¹/₄ cup heavy cream

In a double boiler, heat all ingredients over low heat, stirring occasionally until melted and glaze is perfectly smooth. Cool before using.

And finally . . . putting the *gâteau opéra* all together!
    Using a serrated bread knife and a ruler, cut the *biscuit joconde* into four equal rectangles, about 3¹/₂×10 inches. Place a cake rectangle on a 3×10-inch cake board or tray. Brush with Grand Marnier syrup. Then with a knife, spread on one-third of the *crème au beurre au café*. Place second layer of cake, brush with Grand Marnier syrup, spread on all of the *ganache*. Place third layer, brush with syrup, spread on one-third of the *crème au beurre au café*. Place fourth layer, brush with syrup, spread with rest of the *crème au beurre*. Refrigerate for an hour to harden the *crème au beurre*. Remove cake from the fridge and pour the room-temperature *glaçage au chocolat* over the *gâteau*. With a large metal spatula, smooth the top in one stroke, letting the excess *glaçage* run down over the sides. Return to refrigerator.
    One-half hour before serving, remove the *gâteau* from the refrigerator. Dip the serrated bread knife blade in hot water, then wipe quickly. Trim the sides to remove the uneven patches of glaze to reveal the layers of cake and buttercream. *Et voilà . . .* Praises upon you!

Place des Vosges

rue des Francs-Bourgeois, Paris 04
Metro: St-Paul, Hôtel-de-Ville

Get off the metro and you will walk up the stairs to a carrousel in the middle of rue de Saint-Antoine, just as it changes names from the rue de Rivoli, where you will find a pâtisserie directly behind the carrousel. Jeanette and Georgette always need a pastry to provide courage for locating either the Jewish quarter or the place des Vosges—it's easy to get lost . . . believe it! So. Stop first at the easy-to-find

Aux Désirs de Manon

129, rue Saint-Antoine, Paris 04
Telephone: 01.42.72.32.91
Metro: St-Paul
Closed: Sundays

You will be thankful that you have sustenance from this shop with nothing under an "8." Your choices will be the first *mille-feuilles* that Georgette had seen this year without frosting (of course they never used to have frosting in the good old days, just a dusting of powdered sugar) for €2, a *tarte mendiante* (a mixture of whole nuts in a caramel sauce) for €3, *des soufflés aux pommes, aux abricots* (apple and apricot soufflés), a *tartlette au citron* (lemon tart) topped with very thin slices of lemon for €2.80, and all kinds of cake and puff pastry treasures that you can take with you to eat on the steps of one of the many museums in this *quartier*, or on the bench in the center of Place des Vosges. J. et G. chose a *tartlette à l'orange* for €2.80 because they had never seen one before.

From the pastry shop, Jeanette and Georgette think the best way to find Place des Vosges is to walk straight north (away from the Seine) on rue Pavée for two or three blocks, and then ask! The Place des Vosges is the oldest and, some say, the most beautiful square in Paris. It was certainly the best address in the 15th century. There is a square of thirty-six symmetrical pavilions (nine on each side) constructed with red and gold brick-and-stone-facades with steep slate roofs, designed in the early 15th century. Jeanette says to tell you dear readers that if you get ever close to the pavilions, you will notice that the bricks are a marvelous *trompe-l'oeil* (illusion). The facades are made of plaster and lathing, then painted to look like brick! Victor Hugo lived in the Place des Vosges, where his home at 6, Place des Vosges is now a museum. The Picasso Museum with the largest collection of his work in the world is nearby, as is the charming Musée Coqnacq-Jay with 19th-century paintings, decorative arts, and furniture in their period settings.

While hunting the delicious in the Marais, Georgette noticed that several of the pastry shops of a few years ago had been converted into other kinds of shops. In the past ten years, the area has changed from residential to commercial boutiques, which means very expensive real estate. Some closed pâtisseries had a sign on them that said *"Fermeture Définitive."* Jeanette didn't have to tell Georgette that that means a final closing! Now. Not for your sweet tooth, but for the sweet life of an art historian's perspective and spirit of Paris, you will want to look closely at the shops in the Marais and find, as Georgette and her brother John found, an Italian men's clothing store at 29, rue des Francs-Bourgeois and rue Pavée. The paintings on glass of the old *boulangerie-pâtisserie* were exquisitely restored and conserved with roses at the top and bottom of the gold frames, and, typical of early 1800s' pastry shops, you will see a painting of a flour mill with a waterwheel and shafts of wheat. This particular one is signed "Albert—Décorateur, 88, rue Didot, 14th arr." Oh, Paris! Even with modern and economic changes, the value of the beautiful is conserved.

J. *et* G. always visit the Jewish quarter when they go to this area, especially for the Yiddish *pâtisseries* of Sacha Finkelsztajn.

About four fascinating blocks from the Place des Vosges, and from the same metro stop, you will find

Sacha Finkelsztajn
27, rue des Rosiers, Paris 04
Telephone: 01.42.72.78.91
Metro: St-Paul, Hôtel-de-Ville
Closed: Saturdays, Mondays,
Tuesdays; mid-July through mid-
August; 1–3 pm

Georgette thought this shop was *always* closed, because she had tried several times around 2 PM. Finally there when they were open, Jeanette said, "If it's Jewish, we must try their *vatrouchka*" (cheesecake), and Georgette said, "If you're from New York City, that would be silly!" But. At this pâtisserie you can buy Jewish rye, pumpernickel, and onion bread, as well as pastries of dried fruits such as figs and dates, apples, and raisins and honey. Strudels and poppy-seed cakes cover the shelves. Looking everything over carefully, and realizing that they had not tasted a date since arriving a month ago in Paris, J. *et* G. chose the *roulé aux dattes*, a wonderful rolled sponge cake filled with dried dates. They carried it to the Place des Vosges, walking past the elegant silver ships, antique shops, and chic fashion boutiques on the way. The intense July heat hurried them past the shops to a bench in the shade, in the center of the

Place, where they opened their pastry from the most outstanding Jewish pastry shop in all of Paris and yummmm, it hit the spot! As they looked at the matching pavilions, Jeanette once again explained to Georgette about the *trompe-l'oeil* of the facades.

Before leaving the Jewish quarter, you must look in Jo Goldenberg's restaurant, on rue des Rosiers, even if it isn't lunch or dinner time. If your trip to Paris has left you hungry for chicken soup, chopped liver, gefilte fish, pastrami, or corned beef on rye, Goldenberg's is the only place to go. Open from 8:30 AM to 11 PM, closed Friday afternoon and Saturday, *voici le numéro de téléphone:* 01.48.87.20.16, and the metro is still St-Paul or the Hôtel-de-Ville.

Only one thing left to do. This is the place to buy Jewish holiday greeting cards *en français*, which J. et G. always get a kick out of, to have on hand to send to Jewish friends back in the U.S.A.

Parc Monceau
blvd de Courcelles, Paris 17
Telephone: 01.42.94.08.08
Metro: Monceau
Open: Dawn to dusk

You've picnicked in the Luxembourg Gardens and the Tuileries? You want to try something new, in a chic Paris

neighborhood? If you are lucky enough to be in Paris during school months, choose a Wednesday afternoon, when mothers, fathers, or nannies pick up their young children at school at noon and take them to the 18th-century Parc Monceau to play. You will see children in sand boxes, on roller blades and skateboards, on tricycles, and of course, many more just gleefully running around. You can sit facing lovely formal gardens or a mountain cascade, you can gaze at one of the six Belle Epoque monuments of French writers and musicians, or sit by the Corinthian colonnade at the edge of a small lily pond with baby ducks swimming about.

Begin your trip by taking the metro to Villiers and walking past the carrousel to rue de Lévis, where you will find Jeanette and Georgette's favorite open market in Paris. Open markets are great shopping attractions, especially this one in such a chic arrondissement. Butchers and fruit, vegetable, and cheese vendors hawk their perfectly ripened cheeses, freshest calves' liver and whole rabbits, and, oh, the sweetest strawberries (in season, *bien sûr!*) you'll ever taste. Notice how the French women shop in the open market. You will see that they are very particular, and no French woman ever carries home a bigger piece of meat or fish than she had in mind

to buy. Also notice how neatly and calmly they wait in line for their bread, pastry, or cheese. Listen to the vendors; even if you don't know French, the sound of their voices announcing prices and special products is very distinctive in Paris markets. That beautiful French intonation pervades the air and adds to the market ambience. On display in-between the food vendors are leather goods, kitchenware, shoes, dresses, and perfume, all on tables or racks in the street.

A post office is nearby, where Georgette always runs to buy another aerogram (much cheaper than sending postcards) while Jeanette takes a leisurely coffee at the tea salon on the corner of rue de Lévis and rue Legendre. They

eat their pastry carried from 41, rue de Lévis and order a coffee to enjoy at an outdoor table in the March sun. What lazy fun just watching people strolling by and others marketing. Of course they had to pay extra because they had agreed at last to sit down for their coffee. The market is closed from noon until 2 PM, so don't plan to buy your picnic if you arrive after noon! The street also has a Monoprix which rivals any Woolworth's store you've ever been in. There is a *vaissellerie* with all of the French whiteware, a branch of the same store found on boulevard Raspail.

It's easy to find a pastry, as rue de Lévis has many excellent pastry shops. Tourtière de Gascogne at 21, and Finesse at 25, rue de Lévis are both shops where J. *et* G. have bought many pastries, but their Parc Monceau favorite is the pâtisserie closest to the tea salon:

Boulangerie-Pâtisserie D. Polin
41, rue de Lévis, Paris 17
Telephone: 01.47.63.05.05
Metro: Villiers
Closed: Sundays pm, Mondays

A most elegant shop, as the 17th arrondissement borders the 16th, and the Parc Monceau area is one of the most expensive neighborhoods of Paris in which to live. Here you will find a *chocolatier et glacier* for your favorite ice cream as well. Even though the *mille-feuilles* looked like a "9 + + + ", and the *puits d'amour* were tempting, J. *et* G. chose for the second time a *tulipe*, a tart of pastry cream topped with chocolate and Cointreau.

The *noisette* was also a close choice. A *noisette* is a meringue-based tart with a hazelnut buttercream top. Don't leave Paris without a taste of this irresistible combination of crisp nut meringue with a rich, smooth buttercream filling, topped with a dusting of sugar and often served with a hazelnut coffee sauce. If you are staying in a hotel, go to the Monoprix for paper plates, napkins, and plastic forks and spoons, so that you can enjoy a

pastry with a sauce when you are back at your hotel for *un peu de repos* (a little rest) before your next Parisian adventure.

Don't forget that you are on your way to Parc Monceau to watch and listen to the school children play . . . so after you look, choose, and purchase the precise pastry you are in the mood for, head off down the boulevard de Courcelles just to view the magnificent architecture of the mansions of the area on your way to the lovely Parc Monceau. After you've enjoyed your pastry while watching the French with their children and strolled around the formal gardens, leave the *parc* by way of the front gate by the exotic 18th-century tollhouse, where you'll see the wrought-iron gates with lamp posts of the art deco metro stop. It's hard to leave this spot. But *dépêchez-vous* (do hurry along), because as Jeanette and Georgette have learned ever so long ago—you'll be back!

Seine-à-Seine:
A Fourteen-Metro-Stop Special Pastry Line

Something like a pie-eating contest. Or a Ben & Jerry's ice-cream-eating contest. For those adventuresome and competitive souls who want to travel delicious metro stop to delicious metro stop to see and eat the Paris that few tourists (including French tourists!) get to experience, Jeanette and Georgette propose that you try their "Seine-à-Seine Pastry Line." Looking at the metro map as you enter the metro station, you will see that Line 10 begins just inside the western edge of the left bank and ends at Jussieu, a student hangout where a large medical university is located, on the eastern edge of the Seine. Two of the stops (Odéon and Cluny) will be in the center of the 6th arrondissement, on boulevard St-Michel (boul' Mich', as the students call it) in the Latin Quarter, but the other dozen stops will be new to most of you. Begin anywhere in the city and take the metro to Javel—Line 10.

If there is a sign on a pastry shop that says "*fermeture annuelle*," it means it is closed for the annual three- or four-week vacation that most Parisians take in August. And a seasoned pastry-hunter knows that many, many pastry shops are closed from noon or 1 PM until 3 PM. Now is a good time to mention that if you are going to take *un petit congé* (a day off) from your pastry hunt, make it a Monday. It is fair to say that 90 percent of the pastry shops are closed from Sunday noon until Tuesday morning. The French buy their Sunday pastry in the morning, and bake *crêpes* at home or eat their perfectly ripened fruit on Mondays. It must be said that they *never* go without a dessert . . . *jamais*!

Stop #1: Javel

When you get off the metro that honors the industrialist and car manufacturer André Citroën (1878–1935), you will find two exits. Exit 1, quai André Citroën, has a pleasant little triangle with fruit trees, forsythia, benches, a newspaper stand, and a terrific view of the Eiffel Tower. Exit 2 is on the rue de la Convention. At the top of exit 2, there is a sign directing you to even or odd numbers of rue de la Convention and an area map showing Gare de Paris Javel, Eglise St-Christophe de Javel, Pont Mirabeau, and the Imprimerie Nationale. At 39, rue de la Convention is a monument to the Loge Gutenberg, where the Bible was first printed in French. The only pastry shop left at this stop is Chas. Banette, a chain of bread and pastry shops found all over Paris.

Jeanette *et* Georgette decided to skip the pastry and have an early lunch at Café Régalia, a very busy workman's café—not an American in sight, authentic as you will find—with a beef *bourguignon* "menu" for €12 and a green salad with that always-perfect French vinaigrette dressing for €6. Of course they knew it would be too much food for pastry-hunters and so they split the *plat du jour* and salad, just as you will want to do! Dear readers, do not underestimate the treasure of a neighborhood restaurant outside of the first eight arrondissements! When you find one that is crowded with working Parisians, give it a try. Alone or with friends, the environment of energy and life is entertainment not to be matched for the tourists! Don't miss out on the adventure of finding your own authenticity while out on your pastry hunts in Paris.

And now for dessert, they went back to the Chas. Banette (across from the metro stop) for the best-looking dessert in the place; they chose a *chausson aux pommes*, a large, flaky, apple turnover.

Chausson aux Pommes

Pâte feuilletage (puff pastry)—the basic turnover pastry dough always used for *bouchées, vol-au-vent, fleurons, feuilletés, mille-feuilles* and *palmiers*—is made of flour, ice water, and layers of cold butter folded in so that when baked, the pastry flakes by layers. You can see the tissue-thin layers in a perfect puff pastry. In a *chausson aux pommes,* this puff pastry is cut in the shape of a scallop shell, about 3 inches across, and filled with sliced apples, butter, cinnamon, and nutmeg. Crunchy and dry, the fine layers of pastry crumbs will fall into your lap as you bite into the warm, delightful apple filling.

Wrapped pastry in hand and wished a *bonne journée,* Jeanette *et* Georgette headed down the street toward the Imprimerie Nationale to see what the National Printing buildings looked like. They walked past the St-Christophe Church of Javel. *Zut!* (Darn!) The steps were already taken. As they walked, their warm pastry called out the gastronomic juices in their bodies and souls to hurry and find a suitable eating place! Arriving at the printing buildings, they saw just the right bench in a green park in front, but they weren't let in! For workers only. Looking around, Jeanette spotted a small park directly across the street with four benches, the shortest sliding chute you'll ever see, and a gazebo with thatched roof for children to play in. Sitting in the sun, with the sounds of children's play and laughter nearby, J. *et* G. joyfully unwrapped their still-warm pastry. Ahhhhhhh *parfait!* They experienced the flakiest crust and cooked apple with perfect seasoning—not too sweet, with a touch of nutmeg. With the intention of eating half of her half because they had just eaten lunch and their *après-midi* pastry-tasting had only just begun, Georgette followed her first bite with a second and third . . . it was *so* light. Jeanette gave the *chausson aux pommes* a "9+ ," Georgette a

"10"—how could it be improved? It couldn't! Jeanette, a demanding school teacher who had the highest standards for her "French Vs," was quickly persuaded to raise the grade to a 10. Yeaaaa! Another 10!

Now to find a coffee. They reluctantly left their peaceful spot in the sun in search of the liveliest café for coffee or Coke or tea which, as usual, they found next to the metro stop. J. *et* G. stood at the bar of La Régalia for their *café* (black coffee—espresso—€1.10 at the bar), while complete satisfaction washed over them from their sensational pastry-line beginning.

Leaving La Régalia and walking toward the metro entrance, they unexpectedly spotted the Tour Eiffel in the distance (from the other metro exit not taken). Oh boy! This is Paris. It's so exciting to continue on to the next taste of the pastry line, anticipating the thrilling sights and flavors it will hold.

Stop #2: Charles Michels

There are two metro exits. Exit 1 leads out to place Charles Michels, where you will be delighted to find a carrousel in the square, benches, and a flower stall. Exit 2 leads to rue des Entrepreneurs. At first, Jeanette and Georgette thought that the carrousel was the ideal place to eat a pastry, which is after

all, a major part of enjoying it. But then, as they looked around, it was a little too honky-tonk for them, so they relentlessly continued their search for both the pastry and the place to eat it. The closest pâtisseries were too ordinary, but soon, if you keep left on the corner of rue St-Charles and rue de l'Eglise, you will find, as they did, a very beautiful shop with a long bread line (the first clue for a good pastry):

Boulangerie-Pâtisserie Eric Brunet
105, rue St-Charles, Paris 15
Telephone: 01.40.59.84.70
Metro: Charles Michels
Closed: Sundays, Mondays

This shop is a small place with two stools and a very tiny coffee bar with every pastry looking like an "8" or above. J. *et* G. loved the *profiteroles,* three small cream puffs filled with a custard or vanilla ice cream and smothered with a hot dark chocolate sauce. Most Americans have eaten a *profiterole,* but the French set the standard of excellence—their puffs are lighter and crispier, the cream richer, and the chocolate darker! It's a tough pastry "to go." Sit at the little counter to enjoy your *profiteroles.* Take your coffee right there. Or, wait like Georgette, who always takes her coffee at the café closest to the metro stop where the neighborhood Parisians are standing at the bar for their coffee. Walking back toward the metro on the second stop of the Seine-à-Seine run for pastries, you will have the added thrill of seeing the Eiffel Tower loom before you as you stop at Le Linois for your "stand up" coffee at the *zinc* (bar) for €1.15, or take a table for a coffee at €2.30.

J. *et* G. have learned that it's good to become acquainted with all of Paris. You never know when you'll be in the neighborhood again, when you might not have time to focus on where to find the best pastry. You'll already know and can think of other things. Just for an example, Jeanette and Georgette were cleaning the refrigerator in Françoise's apartment because Georgette's brother John, from the Netherlands, was to visit for the weekend. In a hurry to get on with the pastry hunt rather than doing tedious housework, Georgette inadvertently broke the glass shelf in the *frigo* (refrigerator). Françoise was away for the weekend but coming back on Monday. They hurried out to the 18th-arrondissement appliance stores to ask about a piece of replacement glass. "*Non.*" Not even with the model number, year, size, could they find the proper glass shelf. But, "Go to this number, at Port Javel, on the Seine, where the

warehouses are, and you will find one." The three started out, Georgette promising brother John some wonderful pastries if he would only accompany them on this excursion. Hot. It's July. They walked way beyond the metro stop at Quai Javel in the unfamiliar territory of hi-tech places, with men in white coats shaking their heads *"non"* before Jeanette even asked! Finally, "Go to such-and-such a hardware store near Charles Michels in the 15th, where they will cut you exactly what you want." They hopped on the metro *encore.* . . . Out on Charles Michels, lo and behold, Jeanette and Georgette recognized the carrousel, the benches, the flower stall, and *voilà!* They knew precisely where to get their pastry while they waited for the glass shelf to be cut. A major disaster saved by a perfect pastry in familiar territory.

Stop #3: Emile Zola

When you get off the metro, notice that the two exits are (1) avenue Emile Zola, and (2) rue du Commerce. Take exit 1, to avenue Emile Zola just to think about the great classics author of *L'Assommoir* and the Rougon-Macquart series of *Le Rêve et La Terre*. Georgette's son Ned is a great fan of Zola and has read them all, *en français, bien sûr!* Think about all that you have read or heard about the great Zola with his descriptions of the French working class, the privileged class, the priest who goes astray, the underbelly of Paris at Les Halles, as you take your first right off Emile Zola onto rue du Commerce. There, at number 54, you will find the best pâtisserie in the area, with a very friendly *patron*.

Boulangerie-Pâtisserie Societé Bourlier-Chamignon
54, rue du Commerce, Paris 15
Telephone: 01.45.79.78.07
Metro: Emile Zola
Closed: Sundays pm, Mondays

Wonderfully large *éclairs* and *noix-noisettes* for €2, huge cakes with cream, and *tartes tatin* and *tartes chocolates* for €2.50, offer the best value in pastry shops J. *et* G. have seen. Everything in this small shop was above an "8" in appearance. Besides pastries, they sell olive oil and herbs. Olive oil from southern France, especially La Provence, is what every Parisian seeks; none of the Italian or Greek olive oils for the francophile! For the business people and MBA students among *Paris by Pastry* readers, do walk up rue du Commerce for five blocks to see rue Entrepreneur as it crosses Commerce!

If you are hungry for lunch, or thirsty for your after-pastry coffee, walk a few doors down to

Le Café du Commerce S. Bronet
51, rue du Commerce, Paris 15
Telephone: 01.45.79.78.07
Metro: Emile Zola
Closed: Mondays

J. *et* G. are in their instruction mode, and so it's a good time to say that you can't always tell the name of a pastry shop. The owners' names may be on the awning, but you will often find "Banette" (artisan bakery for quality breads) and almost always, "Boulangerie-Pâtisserie," and sometimes another name not even related to ownership. It is not unusual for Jeanette and Georgette to stand there looking at three different names and trying to figure out what to call the place. Go by the address! At this corner, only Nicolas, the wine store chain, separates the pâtisserie from the metro. Oh, you haven't had your coffee yet? Right next to the metro entrance is Le Sélect, with a yellow awning (and *oui*, a pinball machine), a wonderful-looking café for lunch. As authentic as you can get, with a neighborhood clientele. Order the *steak-frites* (steak and fries) for €10, or the *plat du jour*—for example, the *confit de canard* (thin slices of duck) with wine *(le vin ordinaire, bien sûr)*—for €12. *N'oubliez pas* (don't forget) that coffee is half the price while standing at the bar.

Stop #4: La Motte-Picquet-Grenelle

Keep to the right for your exit; you'll see an overhead subway track and station. One block from the metro you will find two choice pâtisseries. You'll have to choose between them, unless you are a lot hungrier on your fourth Seine-à-Seine stop than J. *et* G. were!

Le Primerose
64, avenue de la Motte-Picquet, Paris 15
Telephone: 01.42.73.32.66
Metro: La Motte-Picquet-Grenelle
Closed: Mondays

The first shop, Le Primerose, has very beautiful pastries: small, rich, with a lot of varying shades of chocolate. But before you make your decision, look next on your walk back to the metro, at

A la Petite Marquise Fenet Pâtissier
50, avenue de la Motte-Picquet, Paris 15
Telephone: 01.47.34.94.03
Metro: La Motte-Picquet-Grenelle
Closed: Mondays

You will find this shop another one that is in the "8 + "-and-above category for sheer number of pastries and showcase presentation. If you long for a chocolate specialty, choose a *mogador* (a dense chocolate cake laced with raspberry and coated with bitter cocoa), an *opéra* (fine slices of almond-flavored cake with layers of coffee and chocolate-truffle cream), a *vendôme* (a chocolate-hazelnut shortbread base with a thick layer of chocolate mousse, iced with a thin layer of dark chocolate). Or you may be all chocolated-out and prefer a Bavarian pastry such as an *arlequin* (a cake laced with kirsch and covered with a pistachio cream), a *clafoutis aux poires* (similar to the heavenly *puits d'amour*, this pastry tart holds slices of pear covered with caramelized *crème chiboust*), a *miroir aux cassis* (a Bavarian cream covered with fresh *cassis*), a berry dessert in season, or even one of their sublime *charlottes*.

Consider these two fabulous pastry shops and choose your favorite! Even though it may seem an impossible task, that's just the kind of impossibility that *Paris by Pastry* wants to provide.

Stop #5: Ségur

C'est facile! (It's easy!) There is only one *sortie* (exit) from this metro. Avenue de Suffren is on the border between the 15th and the 7th arrondissements. (The 7th gets over into the Eiffel Tower and Invalides area. Napoleon Bonaparte's tomb is in the 7th, in the Hôtel des Invalides, under the golden dome of the Sun King's

Dome Church.) Walk straight back opposite the Tour Eiffel toward the elevated metro, one-half block to a most superlative bread shop and pâtisserie:

Le Moulin de la Vierge
166, avenue de Suffren, Paris 15
Telephone: 01.47.83.45.55
Metro: Ségur
Closed: Sundays pm, Mondays

This shop has two other locations in Paris (105, rue Vercingétorix, and 82, rue Daguerre—both in the 14th arrondissement) and it even has brownies and cupcakes just in case you miss the American look

of things after a few days of puffs and creams.

Françoise would approve of this pastry shop in the 15th arrondissement because it specializes in macaroons. Jeanette finally got to choose her favorite flavor, coffee, and with no argument from Georgette, who doesn't even like coffee pastries except for Parisian macaroons. There were several honey pastries, including a *carré miel* (square of nuts, raisins and honey), and this is one of the few places that makes and serves *les cannelés de bordeaux*. Just to demonstrate their high standards for the best ingredients was a large sign in the window: *"Notre Pâtisserie est garantie Pur Beurre"* (pure butter guaranteed). Do pick up a business card before you leave; you'll enjoy the art-deco illustration—a signature piece of many Parisian pastry shops. Always looking for a special reason to choose a pastry, J. *et* G. chose *les cannelés de bordeaux,* simply because they'd never heard of them, and their Parisian friend Françoise is originally from Bordeaux. You will find information about the special corrugated (*cannelés*) molds on page 117. If you want to impress your friends with an uncommon *pâtisserie,* here's your chance! It reminds J. *et* G. of a *financier.*

Les Cannelés de Bordeaux

15 ounces (almost 2 cups) milk
$1/4$ teaspoon vanilla
1 tablespoon butter
2 eggs plus 2 egg yolks
1 tablespoon rum
$1^1/2$ cups white sugar
1 scant cup all-purpose, unsifted white flour

Mix sugar, flour, rum, and melted butter. Stir in the lightly beaten eggs. Bring the milk to a boil and pour over the sugar-and-flour mixture. Add the vanilla and mix well. Let the mixture sit for a few hours in a cool place.

Preheat the oven to 425°F. Fill the silicone molds $3/4$ full and place in the lower part of the oven. Reduce heat to 400°F and bake for one hour. The *cannelés* should be well cooked and look quite dark. Remove from the molds while hot to cool on a rack.

Stop #6: Duroc

Every metro stop has a terrific pastry shop within two blocks on this metro line—*c'est Paris!* The Duroc stop is in the corner of three arrondissements: the 15th, the 7th, and the location of this shop, the 6th (the Latin Quarter). Once again, you will be able to spot the Eiffel Tower in the distance, although this fascinating little niche in the 6th arrondissement is well beyond the tourist trade, even in mid-July at the height of the tourist season. There are two *sorties*; go out to 1, boulevard du Montparnasse, where you will find the Pâtisserie Mirabelle. Please notice! The Mirabelle is across the street from the wine store chain Nicolas. Whenever you are at a loss as to where to go next, look for a Nicolas or the grocery chain Félix Potin, and almost always, there

Tarte aux Mirabelles

This yellow- and amber-cherry tart begins with a *pâte brisée*, the dough used for lining a fruit tart; the pastry cream is spread evenly over the pastry base before arranging the whole, pitted mirabelles on top. One of the pastry problems in America is that restaurants must refrigerate their fruit tarts, a "sanitation law" that the French wouldn't dream of having, knowing that such a cold custom would ruin both the flavor and texture of their pastry perfections.

will be an extraordinary pastry shop next door.

Pâtisserie Mirabelle

1, blvd du Montparnasse, Paris 06
Telephone: 01.47.83.75.39
Metro: Duroc
Closed: Sundays and Mondays; no annual vacation—open all year

At the Mirabelle you will find very big *éclairs*, beautiful fruit tarts just heaped with berries, a *mille-feuilles* (napoleon) topped with almonds, and a *soufflé au citron* that looked beyond temptation. Because of its name, J. *et* G. went with the *tarte aux Mirabelles.*

Besides pastries, the Mirabelle does a very brisk business of quiches, salads and sandwiches. There are a couple of dozen stools with a narrow, marble counter where you can savor your after-pastry coffee. By now, you know that Jeanette and Georgette prefer to take their coffee at the café next door, Le François Coppée. They were so taken with this sleek, modern, upscale Le François Coppée, that they returned the following week for their morning *café et tartine.* Jeanette likes routine, so to move her from her usual 18th-arrondissement café near their apartment, you know it had to be *très spécial!* They arrived around 9 AM, and Georgette picked up a *Herald Tribune* for €2 from the newsstand woman on the street (while Jeanette read her news in French for free from the newspapers hanging on a hook at the bar). J. *et* G. remembered their first visit to the Coppée, before it was renovated, when they couldn't find the newspaper woman to pay for the papers. After looking around, there she was—big as life, playing the pin ball machine in the Coppée! The street cleaners, as they are every morning, were out front washing down the Paris streets with brooms and a stream of water, while the *patrons* were busy cleaning windows and writing menus (announcing the day's specials) on their storefront windows. J. *et* G. no more than got comfortable at their table when they were asked to move. The potato man had arrived, and had to go through the basement trap door beneath their table! Finally settled, J. *et* G. enjoyed their *tartine et café crème*. (Remember that *café crème* is made with milk, never cream, and that the French have milk in their coffee only before 10 AM; after 10 AM, coffee means black. And coffee also means espresso.) Do you know what a *tartine* is? It's a baguette sliced lengthwise and slathered with butter. J. *et* G. like it much more than a croissant, and order *une tartine à partager* (one to share). You know what comes next . . . a pastry every two hours!

Stop #7: Vaneau

There is only one exit to take when you come out of the metro. Take a right, and a right again on rue Vaneau. Enjoy the elite residential look of the street while walking toward rue de Babylone until you find 56, rue Vaneau, a corner shop.

**Peltier Père et Fils
Azrak**
56, rue Vaneau, Paris 07
Telephone: 01.45.48.98.16
Metro: Vaneau
Closed: 1:30 to 3:30 pm daily;
Mondays; August

Here you will find a magnificent original pâtisserie marble counter, a wonderful painted ceiling of roses, and not-so-wonderful pastries. If you have French-Canadian cousins or friends, they will be thrilled to know that the Montreal shop has a branch in Paris! After checking out the original interior, J. *et* G. advise you to save your appetite for 44, rue de Babylone.

The Vaneau stop is so full of surprises that it's hard to know where to begin. Surprises in opposites, really. In the very heart of Paris's 7th arrondissement, we were innocently walking along toward rue de Babylone from Vaneau, seeing only very old, high stone walls and beautiful rooftops, which reminded Jeanette and Georgette of Connecticut and Rhode Island's walled estates. We wondered where these elite French bought their pastries until we took a left on Babylone and found

Claude Binet
44, rue Babylone, Paris 07
Telephone: 01.47.05.44.66
Metro: Vaneau
Closed: Sundays

There are several tables at which to eat your pastry and have a coffee, and you will notice, as you check out the sparkling glass shelves that hold the pastry treasures, that many locals of this residential area are seated and having a *café* with their friends. J. *et* G. know you'll agree: this is a perfect place to sit down and talk over the wonders of stalking the sweet life on the streets of Paris.

Georgette wanted to select two pastries so that they could describe more for their dear readers. Jeanette wanted no more pastries because it was so late in the day and they had heard of a nearby restaurant off Vaneau. G. hesitated over a *bombe-amande*, a chocolate tart that looked terrific for €2.50, and the *St-Claude*, a dome-shaped little cake made of passion-fruit-soaked wedges with chocolate in between and a chocolate covering over the dome, but she felt most like the *tarte aux noix,* a walnut custard with walnuts on top. Something more simple would be the wonderful-looking tarts, *citron* or *chocolat* for €2.60, or a *religieuse* for €2.50. But *non,* standing there studying her options, finally Georgette asked for the *vénus,* a *pêches rôties au caramel noisettine*—peaches in nutty caramel—that G. had never seen before and of course just had to try.

Pêches Rôties au Caramel Noisettine

A combination of hazelnuts, pistachios, caramel, and peaches, this pastry ought to be tried when you are ravishingly hungry because it is so ravishingly rich and filling! The caramel is prepared by cooking sugar and butter over a low heat until it is golden. A drop of grenadine is added. Whole peaches are blanched in boiling water, skins removed, before being baked with the caramel and hazelnuts for 10 minutes. Pistachio nuts are split and studded in the top of the peaches, while the caramel and hazelnut mixture forms a glaze. Georgette recommends that you eat this pastry in the shop, as it works ever so much better with a spoon.

After a tasting for a rating, the two francophiles continued down rue Babylone, where a mirage appeared before their eyes. Looking at each other because they couldn't take it in (even Jeanette had never heard of it in all her years of accompanying her students to Paris), there, before their very unbelieving eyes, stood a Chinese pagoda sitting in a garden! They hurried across the street to 57, rue de Babylone, where, underneath the wild-looking tree that looked as old as China shading a huge, front portion of it, they discovered the neighborhood cinema! Upon inquiring where on earth it could have come from, they learned, *en français, bien sûr,* that long ago, in the 19th century (1869, to be exact—you art historians know, as the rest of us don't, that Oriental art was *la mode* at that time and adopted by many of the French artists of the day), Monsieur Alexandre Marcel, a director of the first department store of Paris, Au Bon Marché, built this pagoda for his wife because she adored everything Oriental and he adored her! The building—the stained glass windows, the prints, and even the sculptured wooden framework— came directly from Japan. After it was closed in 1928, the Chinese Ambassador rented it in 1930. In 1931 La Pagode became a theatre for foreign films. It is now a cinema specializing in classical films and films with strong images of Paris. Go! See the red plush seats, original chandeliers, stained glass windows, Oriental panels, sculptures, and a period room all in one magnificent place. The price of the movie is worth the price of being in the Pagoda.

Digesting such a visual treat and history whetted the appetites of J. *et* G. as they retraced their steps back to Vaneau, a few streets away between metro stops Vaneau and Duroc. Rounding the corner, they happily found the restaurant where someone had told them that the price was right . . .

Chez Germaine
30, rue Pierre Leroux, Paris 07
Metro: Duroc, Vaneau
Closed: Sundays

No reservations. No credit cards. No toilets. No coffee. No questions!

We were told that this was a mom-and-pop, traditional home-cooking place. The first time we arrived, Jeanette asked, *"Où sont les toilettes, s'il-vous-plaît?"* (The French always use toilet in the plural, J. explained to G.)

"We do not have toilets, Madame."

Unbelieving, G. exclaimed, "But you are a restaurant—you have to have a toilet!"

"We do not have toilets,

Madame."

"Where do your customers go who need a toilet?"

"We do not have toilets, Madame. They go down the street to a big restaurant, Madame."

Whereupon J. got up and left while G. looked around and thought, "If there is no wine or beer here, we're leaving!

"Madame, avez-vous du vin rouge ordinaire et de la bière?"

"Bien sûr!"

A menu was produced with *steak-frites, plat du jour, et dessert du jour—tarte tatin. Très facile* (easy)! J. returned with a glass of red wine waiting for her on the table, and a beef stew with root vegetables on its way. We then learned that coffee was also down the street. In the meantime, most everyone who walked in were regulars, and there was *no* conversation between Madame and the regulars. Most ordered the *plat du jour.* Believe us when we say, it's truly a French experience and the price is right!

Stop #8: Sèvres-Babylone

There are three exits, the first to rue de Velpeau where Au Bon Marché, the oldest department store in Paris (designed by Gustave Eiffel of the Eiffel Tower), is located. But you will take the third exit, odd numbers to rue de Sts-Pères. The stairs will bring you up to where the rue de Sèvres joins

rue de Babylone, on the Square Boucicaut, facing Au Bon Marché. You will see a restored stone wall, beautiful roses in July, many well-dressed children playing in a sand pile, and fabulous architecture all year around. At the end of the park is a marble sculpture of Madame Boucicaut, 1816-1887, lady bountiful of the times, a charitable activist giving to a poor boy and his mother sitting on the step with a baby. This is the wife of M. Boucicaut, who was a well known philanthropist of his time and the director of Au Bon Marché. On one corner of the square is the *très* fashionable hotel, Lutetia, the only *hôtel palace* (luxury) on the south side of the Seine. It is an art deco building with a renowned literary bar where neighborhood publishers hang out. The Bank of France is on another corner.

SIP Babylone
46, boulevard Raspail, Paris 07
Telephone: 01.45.48.87.17
Metro: Sèvres-Babylone
Open: Every day

The SIP pâtisserie on the corner of Babylone stands up to the 19th-century architecture of the apartments seen from this square, and there's a *salon de thé* with tables, a counter, sandwiches, ice cream—the works. J. et G. thought about the *tarte normande,* but they chose a new one for the sake of *Paris by Pastry*: the *conversation*. This pastry has a meringue base and is topped by an almond cream. Jeanette expressed with a sigh that she really didn't think it was anything to converse about. Recently, the SIP Babylone has expanded into much more café and much less pâtisserie, so that J. *et* G. don't go there any more.

There really isn't a decent pâtisserie nearby, although Georgette will give a nod to the Maison du Chocolat, within sight of the square, for those chocolate-lovers who feel that J. *et* G. don't appreciate them enough in their

pastry book. In addition to the beautiful chocolates, there are chocolate *éclairs* for €3.80, a *délice* for €4.60, and especially appealing to Jeanette and Georgette were the chocolate cookies for €3. They hope that their readers notice that these prices are much higher than most *éclairs*, cookies, or a *délice*. That is because French chocolate is of a finer quality (hence higher price), and much less sweet than American chocolate. The French pride themselves on how little sugar they can use in making their cooking chocolate in order to taste the chocolate more and the sugar less.

Georgette knows that there are a lot of guides to Paris restaurants for our dear readers to search. But while they are right here, once more she cannot resist citing her very favorite restaurant in Paris. Whether she is alone hunting the *pâtisseries*, with Jeanette, or with her brother John, she adores L'Epi Dupin, one block away from Au Bon Marché, at 11, rue Dupin, telephone 01.42.22.64.56. Lunch or dinner, you will find an exquisite presentation with a smile, the highest of fresh, seasonal foods, and, best of all, a "22" rating from Zagat, for $44. Georgette knows that if you double the rating, it is usually three times the price or more! Be sure to get reservations— it's a small restaurant.

Stop #9: Mabillon

There's only one *sortie* (exit) at stop #9, with stairs or escalator. (Remember that Jeanette and Georgette always choose the stairs.) You will come out on rue Mabillon (halfway to St- Sulpice). It is surprising to see so little commotion here, just a few short blocks away from the over-run (especially in July and August) St-Germain-des-Prés area. Take your pastry to the Place St-Sulpice, just a city block away. Allow enough time to see the impressive inside of this 16th-century church, featuring mural paintings by Delacroix— don't miss Delacroix's *Jacob Wrestling with the Angel*—and an organ that is considered one of the finest in France. Better yet, go to a concert there, as St-Sulpice is known for its organ concerts year around. If you are there for Holy Week, and many of you "Spring Break" students and teachers will be, you don't have to be Catholic to attend a service. Look in the weekly *Pariscope* (some English translations) or *L'Officiel des Spectacles* (G. prefers the challenge of trying to figure out the French), which come out every Wednesday (purchase at any newsstand), for current movies, concerts, exhibits, lectures, dates, times, and reviews. They are in French, but Jeanette promises that if you've had even two years of high school French, you will be able to figure out the events, times and places. If Georgette can read it, *you* can read it!

Sarl Ladoux
12, rue Mabillon, Paris 06
Telephone: 01.43.54.16.93
Metro: Mabillon
Closed: Mondays

It's an easy hunt to find this lovely *salon de thé* with skillfully prepared meringues, apple-shaped *tartes aux pommes* (apple tarts), and a *duchesse* (a puff pastry base topped with strawberries, and cream to top it off) for €4. The *tarte au citron* had a fine topping of meringue, unusual to see in Paris. And then there was a *Polonaise, a baba chiboust, a prine noir*, and a very flamboyant *mousse aux fraises des bois* (wild strawberry mousse). Beside the delectable pastries are enticing sandwiches.

J. *et* G. have to admit that they were too hungry to eat a sweet right away, and chose instead a perfect *jambon et brie* (ham and cheese) sandwich, with mustard (no butter, no mayo), on densely crusted Poilâne bread. Many cafés have a sign at the bar announcing, "We serve only Poilâne bread." Poilâne started making bread in the traditional wood-fired brick ovens in 1932. The bread is made using only stone-ground flour, water and sea salt. J. *et* G. have hunted, found, and tasted in both their shops (at 8, rue du Cherche-Midi, Paris 06, and 49, boulevard de Grenelle, Paris 15). They shared the perfect sandwich on the steps of St-Sulpice before going on to

Stop #10: Odéon

Whenever Jeanette *et* Georgette plan to see a movie *en français, bien sûr,* they usually end up at Odéon, St-Germain, or Champs-Elysées cinemas. Check the weekly *Pariscope* or *L'Officiel des Spectacles* to get movie programs and dates. Keep in mind that movies on Mondays cost fewer euros.

Vieille France
14, rue Buci, Paris 06
Telephone: 01.43.26.55.13
Metro: Odéon
Closed: Mondays

To find Vieille France, cross boulevard St-Germain and go to the corner of rue de Buci and rue de Seine, the heart of the Latin Quarter and Left Bank tourism. Founded in 1834, this shop is exquisite, each pastry of intricate design and subtle color. You will find a *charlotte* of red fruits with just a drop of red raspberry on the *groseilles à maquereau* (gooseberry), wild strawberry and raspberry tarts, cakes, and a magnificent *St-Honoré.* Jeanette asked about the *coup de soleil,* a shortbread dough filled with cream and caramelized on top, but Georgette thought it

was just too much for the moment. Ready to go to the cinema to see anything with Catherine Deneuve, Georgette knew they could handle something with fruit, so she persuaded Jeanette to try the

Charlotte aux Poires et Fraises du Bois

(Pear and wild strawberry charlotte)
Line a flan ring with a sponge cake. Fill the flan one-quarter full of *meringue italienne* and whipped cream blended together with pear liqueur and gelatin. Scatter pear cubes and wild strawberries over the *charlotte.* Cover the fruit with more cream mixture, scatter the rest of the fruit and cover with a daisy-patterned sponge circle. Cool, remove from the ring, and sprinkle the top with powdered sugar.

Before leaving rue de Buci, find 6, rue de Buci, and you will see superb pastries at Carton, closed on Mondays. The *citron meringue* for €2.40 was as good a piece of lemon meringue pie you've ever had in your life! There were several flavors of *crème brûlée*, and Georgette would match the *religieuse* for €2.10 with any in Paris. Look in on La Bonbonnière de Buci next door, which is open every day. J. *et* G. don't think it's possible that you will like it better than Vieille France and Carton, but then you may end up there on a Monday, and it will look perfectly wonderful to you!

Stop #11: Cluny

Thinking of boul' Mich', the students' name for boulevard St-Michel, Jeanette and Georgette couldn't remember ever seeing a pâtisserie in this student section, the Latin Quarter, home of the Sorbonne (where Jeanette earned *un diplôme*). You will love the bustling area, alive with the two most prestigious *lycées*, and crammed with student bookstores, *boutiques optiques,* students, cafés, jean shops, students, glasses frame shops, movie theatres, students, shoe shops, and jazz clubs stretching from the Seine to the Luxembourg Gardens. *Hélas,* McDonald's and many another fast-food place can be found on boul' Mich'. And oh yes, besides the students, bookstores and cinemas, there is the finest collection of medieval art in the world in a renovated 15th-century ruin, le Musée de Cluny, right on boul' Mich'. Especially known for its tapestries (the Unicorn Series, the best example of *mille-fleurs* style from the 15th century), the Cluny is open from 9:30 AM to 5:15 PM every day except Tuesdays and holidays.

The pastry, the pastry! You must not forget to choose your pastry! Leaving the Cluny metro, Jeanette started asking students where they buy their pastries. They sent the two pastry-stalkers to a shop several blocks away from the Cluny. Walking away from boul' Mich' across rue St-Jacques, keep going until you get to the corner of 35, rue des Ecoles and rue de Jean de Beauvais. You will see a monument to Mihail Eminescu (1850–1889), a poet and philosopher, and *voilà*, you will find a little pâtisserie! Right across the street is the College of France and a monument to the University of Paris.

Pâtisserie Ecoles
38, rue des Ecoles, Paris 05
Metro: Cluny
Closed: Sundays; 3 weeks in August

This pastry shop was filled with huge portions of pastries. (No surprise, *n'est-ce pas?*) You have learned by now that where students gather—and this, after all, is the street of the schools—the pastries get bigger and cheaper. J. *et* G. looked at the *tarte au citron* (€2), pear and almond cake wedges with apple on top, big round cake of almond and orange, and a huge *flan aux fruits* (€1.80). And then they eyed a *super meringue* (a cone-shaped puff of meringue that came in strawberry, pistachio and vanilla—a specialty of this very, very busy shop brimming with students) for €1.60. Georgette began fantasizing that if she were an American student and wanted to meet a French university student, she would surely begin here—standing in line for her *pâtisserie. Comme d'habitude* (as usual), J. *et* G. were the only Americans in there!

Once you have pastry in hand, head back to the entrance of the Cluny Museum, where there is a little courtyard bench on which you can sit immersed in the medieval to enjoy your treat. But if you're looking to relax without learning anything for at least half an hour, then head for Place Paul Painlevé, a tiny rose-garden park that borders rue des Ecoles and Place Paul Painlevé, in back of the Cluny and looking at the Sorbonne. Some of you will have learned all you want to know about the Sorbonne. But for those

pastry-hunters who want even more information about the streets of Paris, here's more than those other readers want to know: La Sorbonne was founded in the 1200s as a theology college, and all the classes were taught in Latin (hence, "the Latin Quarter"). There are free lectures now, open to the public, and you can also visit the gold-domed 17th-century chapel. There. That hardly seems like too much, *d'accord*?

And now, it's back on the metro to

Stop #12: Maubert

There are three exits; you will take the stairs (or escalator) to Exit 2, Place Maubert. When you get off at the top of the escalator at this stop, you will immediately see a huge outdoor market that sells everything from fish, meat, and fruit, to rugs! Right across boulevard St- Germain is the *boulangerie-pâtisserie* that you are hunting for. The shop is opposite a little triangular park with a fountain, two double benches, and a fantastic view of the magnificent Ste-Chapelle spire and the wonderful Parisian rooftops. Jeanette and Georgette often find the spot where they are going to snack on their latest treat well before they have their pastry in hand.

Boulangerie-Pâtisserie
47, boulevard St-Germain,
Paris 05
Telephone: 01.43.54.04.14
Metro: Maubert
Closed: Tuesdays; two weeks in
July and August

There is nothing below a "9" at 47, boulevard St-Germain! J. *et* G. were told by the *patrons* that many Americans come in and that madame can prepare a box of pastries to take home on the plane. The shop is also a *confiserie* (sweets shop), and offers a great array of chocolates and caramel, as well as sandwiches. The sandwiches looked fabulous: a ham and camembert for €3.20, *crudités avec rôti de porc* (raw vegetables with roast pork) for €3.80. J. *et* G. splurged and decided on two pastries that they had never seen before. Georgette really wanted to buy the best-looking *tarte au citron* she has ever seen in her life, but remembered that for the sake of *Paris by Pastry*, she had to sacrifice and try the mango-cassis mousse tart, and the little fig, shaped like a whole fig covered with a green icing. If the weather invites you to eat inside, there is a little table looking out at the fountain and rooftops, so *asseyez-vous*! Otherwise, hurry to the park and enjoy each bite.

Stop #13: Cardinal Lemoine

There are two *sorties* (exits), and the pâtisserie is right there at the top of the stairs—the only exit you will consider.

Banette
Martial Griuet
28, rue Monge, Paris 05
Telephone: 01.43.25.16.09
Metro: Cardinal Lemoine
Closed: Sundays; August

You will find more creams here than anywhere: cream on the *forêt noire* (black forest), cream on the puff pastries, cream on the *opéra*, and cream on the fruit tarts. If this is not your thirteenth pastry today, then you will love this shop and the privilege of selecting the most delectable cream pastry. But for Jeanette and Georgette, the very thought of rich cream after twelve other pastries just didn't wash!

From this shop you can walk up the hill to the Panthéon, or down the hill to the Seine. As Georgette had heard of an Alsatian pâtisserie close by, she decided to walk toward the Seine on rue Cardinal Lemoine, hoping to hunt down this shop after three other pastryless attempts at trying the chef's *madeleines*, for which he is well known.

**Pâtisserie-Biscuiterie
Alsacienne
A. Lerch**
*4, rue du Cardinal Lemoine,
Paris 05
Telephone: 01.43.26.15.80
Metro: Cardinal Lemoine
Closed: Mondays, Tuesdays;
August*

A bread and pastry shop, the
Pâtisserie-Biscuiterie Alsacienne
offers wonderful baguettes and
country breads. Very few pastry
shops have *tarte au fromage blanc*
(cheesecake), but here you will
find it a specialty. Even though
they had heard of his *kougelhopf*—
an Alsatian coffee cake—Jeanette
had *madeleines* on her mind, as the

pastry chef told them that they
were one of his specialties.

This end of rue du Cardinal
Lemoine leads right to the Pont de
la Tournelle, a bridge to the Ile St-
Louis. With one more stop to go
on their Seine-à-Seine pastry hunt,
they certainly didn't have time to
run around the elegant Ile St-
Louis, and they were in no mood
for Berthillon's famous ice cream
shops over there. However, sitting
on the Pont de la Tournelle, the
17th-century classical architecture
was a thrilling sight which they
took time to view. Jeanette says
that on the column of the bridge
stands a statue of Ste-Geneviève,
the patron saint of Paris, watching
over the City of Light. Even
though Georgette couldn't ever
verify that it *is* Ste-Geneviève,
their dear readers realize by now
that Jeanette knows her French
culture! The word is that in 451
AD, when Attila the Hun
conquered large areas of France, a
young maiden, Geneviève,
convinced the people of Paris that
God would protect them, and that
they should not leave the city. Her
prediction came true, and she was
later designated as Ste-Geneviève,
patron saint of Paris. In her honor,
J. *et* G., think it's only her due to
have the cake that honors her
spelled out for the hunters of *Paris
by Pastry*.

Gateau de Ste-Geneviève

1¹/₂ cups flour
1¹/₂ teaspoons baking powder
¹/₂ teaspoon baking soda
¹/₈ teaspoon salt
³/₄ cup sour cream
¹/₂ cup granulated sugar
1 tablespoon rum
¹/₃ cup lemon juice
2 egg yolks
2 egg whites
Pinch of salt
2 tablespoons granulated sugar
Powdered sugar

Preheat oven to 350°F. In a small mixing bowl, stir together the first four
ingredients. In a large mixing bowl, whisk together sour cream, ¹/₂ cup
granulated sugar, rum, lemon juice, and egg yolks. Stir in the flour
mixture and beat just until a smooth batter is formed.

In a deep mixing bowl, beat together the egg whites and pinch of salt
at high speed until soft peaks form. Add 2 tablespoons granulated sugar
and continue beating until stiff. Beat one-third of whites into cake batter,
and then carefully fold in rest of whites. Bake in buttered and floured
9×9-inch baking tin (or do as Georgette does, and use a silicone 9-inch
round pan) for 30 minutes. Cool on a rack. Serve with a topping of
powdered sugar, whipped cream, or your favorite icing. Jeanette readily
admits that she prefers coffee ice cream with her *gâteau de Ste-Geneviève*.

Stop #14: Jussieu

You've come from one side of the Seine, starting at a metro station with a park honoring the Citroën auto industry, to the other side, which is filled with photocopy machines, music stores, students, bookstores, pizzerias, restaurants (Japanese, Arab, Mexican, Lebanese, Vietnamese), and more students everywhere you look. The University of Pierre and Marie Curie medical school is located right at this stop; the Institute of the Arab World, the Mosque, the Mineralogical Museum, and the Arène de Lutèce (a Roman arena from the 2nd century) aren't far away. Jeanette wants you to know that Lutetia was the Roman name, in Latin, meaning "marsh," while the French called it Lutèce. The escalator takes you up to an island swarming with students. Georgette wouldn't go so far as to say that this metro stop is like New York City in its diversity, but then, it isn't typical of Paris, either. *Ah oui!* The *pâtisserie!*

Le Boulanger d'Antan
6, rue Linné Paris 05
Telephone: 01.47.07.10.94
Metro: Jussieu
Closed: Saturdays, Sundays;
August

Don't expect much in the way of French pastries. Diversity in people equals diversity in food, *bien sûr!* There are cakes, breads, ice cream, big Alsatian cobblers, cream puffs, and muffins. This particular pastry shop does wonderful *croissants, cannelés de bordeaux, financiers, éclairs, religieuses,* and fruit tarts. It was July when J. *et* G. were last at this stop . . . they went for a pistachio ice cream. Have you seen the size of a French scoop? *Trop petit ça* (very much too small). Perfect for J. *et* G. They didn't even think of sharing one!

The International Association
of Master Pastry Chefs

When Jeanette *et* Georgette began keeping notes for their *Paris by Pastry* ten years ago, there were eighty master pastry chefs in the whole universe: sixty-two in France—five of them in Paris—and eighteen in the rest of the world. They were selected by the *Association Internationale des Maîtres Pâtissiers* (International Association of Master Pastry Chefs) for the creativity and quality of their *chefs-d'oeuvre* (masterpieces). The raw materials are of the finest—the best butter, cocoa of superior origins—and the chefs have already proven their ability to create refined flavors, soft or crisp textures, harmoniously contrasted colors, all finely joined together to capture the pleasure of the pastry. Jeanette and Georgette couldn't wait to test out all five of these master pastry shops of Paris. Fact-checking and updating is part of the excitement of finding the pastry—the thrill of anticipating the hunt. Of seeing what's new in Paris. Such as the latest *"pâtisserie orientale"* craze.

Just as we were going to press, Georgette hurried over to Paris to check out the master pastry chefs and learned that there is no longer such an association. Disappointed at first, she soon learned that each of the following three shops was sold to a pastry chef of the highest standards. In back of the showcases hung diplomas, the first she had seen, from the *Société des Pâtissiers Français*. These diplomas are given only to the most creative pâtissiers who use the highest quality ingredients. Also impressive to Georgette was the thermometer that varied between 6 and 7 degrees Celsius on the window shelf displaying the pastries at Demoulin. There, too, all of the pastries in the window told what percentage of chocolate or cocoa was used in the particular pastry.

So, although these particular shops are no longer certified by the association, they are certified by Georgette as outstanding in quality, creativity and imagination. Keep in mind that G. knows what she is talking about when it comes to Paris pastries. Remember too, that stalking the new experience, sight,

spirit, and romance on the streets of Paris is your joyous mission. Wait until you find these!

Demoulin
6, boulevard Voltaire, Paris 11
Telephone: 01.47.00.58.20
Metro: République
Closed: Sundays, Mondays; August

When Jeanette and Georgette set out to test the first of the three master pastry chefs in Paris, they took the metro to Place de la République, a Parisian street site where they had never been before. Georgette was *thrilled* at the sight of the dramatic tribute to the Republic of France. The magnificent white marble base by Dalou rises high to record in bronze relief the great events in the revolutionary history of France from its beginning to 1880. Surrounded by lions, the base holds the Morice brothers' bronze Statue to the Republic. French university students love the Place de la République, and if you watch the TV news you will be able to see the students on strike at this very statue every spring.

Oh *oui, la pâtisserie, la pâtisserie* . . . Coming out of the metro to the Place de la République, follow the signs to the statue. Georgette and Jeanette smiled the short distance to 6, boulevard Voltaire to a small, friendly, and very fine pastry and chocolate shop filled with scrumptious "10s" and more! The manager was as gracious as her pastries were good, telling Jeanette about the holiday specialties for *Pâques* (Easter) while Georgette was busy writing in her notebook. Beautifully painted Easter eggs, baby chicks, ducks, fish, and bunnies graced the shelves. Most Parisian families order a *gâteau de Pâques* for their Easter dinner. It is a layer cake made with a *génoise* batter (sugar, eggs, butter, and flour), with very light cream cheese, chantilly cream, and cherry jam, and decorated with fresh cherries.

If you wonder where the tradition of Mardi-Gras ("Fat Tuesday"—Shrove Tuesday) comes from, it's from the French, who always eat *crêpes* (pancakes) the night before Ash Wednesday when *carême* (Lent) begins, which often brings fasting and "giving up" the sweet stuff. Georgette wants to get this point straight right off: There is no comparison between an American pancake and a French *crêpe*! Just for instance, in the French *crêpe*, there are three eggs to one cup of flour. The *crêpes* are paper thin, layered with a sweet or savory topping, and then folded twice into fourths. Françoise, J.'s *et* G.'s friend with whom they often stay, makes wonderful *crêpes suzette*. Once every visit, on a Monday evening when the pâtisseries are closed, she gets out that bottle of Grand Marnier, and Jeanette and Georgette know they are in for a treat! The most fun place for you to buy a *crêpe* will be on the street, just like New York's hot dog stands. You will find both savory and sweet *crêpes* of all flavors and combinations. Don't miss buying one so that you will know firsthand about this French pastry of the Parisian street.

Demoulin specializes in holiday pastries. No family in France would be without the *Bûche de Noël* (Yule log) on Christmas day, seldom made at home but ordered ahead of time from their neighborhood pâtisserie. This is a rolled sponge cake filled with flavored buttercream and covered with Italian meringue that looks like chocolate bark. It is always decorated with woodland trimmings of meringue mushrooms, trailing vines of pale green buttercream, acorns and holly leaves, and a pair of little meringue boots. Jeanette reminds Georgette that Père Noël leaves gifts in children's boots or wooden shoes in France, not in American stockings! *Les Bûches de Noël* are made in flavors of chocolate, coffee, hazelnut, chestnut, and strawberry.

Soon after New Years Day comes January 6th, or Epiphany, when most Europeans open their Christmas gifts, representing the time when the three kings brought gifts to baby Jesus *dans la crèche.* The pastry of this celebration is *La Galette des Rois* (the king's cake). This *galette* always has a hidden bean, and the lucky person who gets the piece of cake with the bean is queen or king for the day! Some pastry chefs and mamas put more than one bean in their Epiphany celebration cake, depending on the number of children in the family.

The pastries at Demoulin that gave every evidence of being "10s," priced between €2.60 and €3.10, were the *ambre* (a layer of praline mousse followed by a layer of chocolate mousse over a sugar pastry, topped with a hazelnut nougat); the *délice* (a layer of vanilla mousse followed by a layer of chocolate mousse over an almond pastry, finished with caramelized cream; the *planteur* (a pastry cream blended with white rum in a pastry tart, topped with pineapple wedges and decorated with cocoa beans); the *guanaja* (70% cocoa, a *biscuit au chocolat,* dome shaped, with a *mousse au chocolat* inside); the *préfet* (a rum-raisin shortbread base with a chocolate topping); the *pâte au chocolat,* the *pomme caramel* (caramelized apple mousse topped with a caramel cream); the *tarte paysanne* (a pastry shell filled with apples and topped with caramelized cream); the *tartelette orange* (a shortbread base topped with an orange caramelized cream); and the *soufflé aux framboises* (raspberry shortbread base topped with cream). After much deliberation, they selected the *symphonie* (a base of hazelnut meringue followed with a layer of chocolate mousse and topped with a coffee mousse). They never tire of watching their beautiful pastry being expertly wrapped in pastry paper without tape or string.

J. *et* G., without verbally agreeing, headed back to that magnificent statue among the lions, and sat on a green bench in the small park to watch the sweet life of Parisians on wheels, whizzing around the Place de la République.

Before leaving the 11th arrondissement, where the Place de la République is located, J. *et* G. want our pastry-hunters to know that the 11th arrondissement is now *au courant* and trendy for the young-professionals and ex-pats sets—brimming with clubs, restaurants, galleries, and wine bars, and the ever-so-fashionable Maghreb pastry shops, such as B. K. And while they are in the neighborhood, our readers will want to profit by going over to the nearby 20th arrondissement, which is probably known best for the Père Lachaise Cemetery (three metro stops away). The Deadheads (followers of the Grateful Dead rock group) flock to Père Lachaise from all over the world because The Doors hero, rock star Jim Morrison, is buried there. The rest of the world knows Père Lachaise for the graves of Proust, Chopin, Sarah Bernhardt, Balzac, and the most popular French singer of the 20th century, Edith Piaf.

On to the second of three master pastry chefs in Paris. Continue on the metro to the Place de la Nation.

Le Triomphe

23, rue du Rendez-vous, Paris 12
Telephone: 01.40.02.08.79
Metro: Place de la Nation
Closed: Sundays, Mondays

Coming up out of the metro, J. *et* G. first spotted the carrousel and then the group of mighty bronze lions pulling a cart on which above them loomed Aimé Jules Dalou's 1883 sculpture of the marvelous *Triomphe de la Republique* in black silhouette against the sky. Whenever Jeanette sees the statues symbolizing the Republic of France, she is always reminded of Marianne. Do you know Marianne? Jeanette has told her French classes for thirty years that Marianne is the "Uncle Sam" of France. She symbolizes the people (unlike Uncle Sam, who symbolizes the government) and is imprinted on the French stamp with a revolutionary bonnet. *C'est ça,* Jeanette?

On either side of avenue du Trône, you will see two magnificent high towers, each with a Roman-looking soldier on top, which originally were the tollgates to Paris. Walk through a beautiful circular garden where you may decide to return to sit on the steps of the monument and watch the traffic swirl around it, or to sit on the green benches at either side of the monument and just enjoy the beauty. If you have young children with you who are too hungry to get to the best, you will see many places to satisfy their immediate hunger until you find excellence. In the Place de la Nation, as all over Paris, you will find excellent *glaciers* (ice cream shops) from France, America, and Italy, and *confiseries* and *chocolatiers* from France and Belgium. On avenue du Trône and in the Place de la Nation there are brasseries for lunch, as well as your after-pastry coffee spots.

But you will find the delicious if you go down rue du Rendez-vous. You'll need a map, or just keep asking for the street. Throughout your *Paris by Pastry* adventures look in the metro station of every stop for the local map, a *plan,* before you get out of the station so you at least have an idea of the layout of the land before you ask directions. You will discover a treasure-triangle with (a) the pâtisserie, (b) the church steps of

Paro Isse de l'Imaculate Conception on which to eat your pastry, and (c) the perfect bar for after-pastry coffee, the Tabac de la Poste. These three important places are just steps away from each other. *Quelle chance* (what luck) for the weary pastry-hunter!

Here are just a few of the specialties from this very select master pastry chef: the *ambassade*, a shortbread pastry base with coffee and vanilla cream, caramelized apples and raisins; the *bagatelle*, a pastry tart filled with vanilla cream, topped with red fruits and a thin layer of gelatin; and the *délice des sous-bois*, two chocolate mousses on a chocolate pastry base. The *tartelette à la rhubarbe* was almost a selection at €2.95. Georgette wanted to take the *helena*, a chocolate pear pastry, back to New York City for her friend Helen, but J. reminded G. that they weren't leaving for a month. The *mozart* was a combination of cassis, passion fruit and raspberries—yummmmm. If it had been later in the day, Jeanette would have chosen the *équinoxe*, a chocolate pastry base covered with a layer of dark chocolate mousse and topped with a pistachio custard cream—in the shape of a hexagon! (Jeanette wants her readers to know that France is shaped like a hexagon. "*Mais alors,*" Georgette retorted. They already knew that.) And of course the *rendez-vous*, a chocolate-based pastry covered with chocolate mousse and topped with a raspberry sauce.

Georgette and Jeanette were looking at a morning first-pastry-of-the-day, and so the *pain aux raisins* (raisin roll) wasn't to be resisted, even though there was also the best-looking *chausson aux pommes* they had ever seen. It was very flaky with a design of a leaf embossed on it. *Mais*, the *pain aux raisins* looked good, and later tasted as good as it looked. It was light in color and texture and simply oozed with custard and raisins. Because they took so long getting there, J. *et* G. decided to try the *financier* as well. Although the *financier* looks like an overcooked bran muffin, it is more like a soft, almond cake-muffin on the inside. It has a crusty, sometimes burned outside which results from starting in a very hot oven, and then baking temperature is reduced to keep the inside soft and moist. These pastries are called *financiers* because they are in the shape of a solid gold brick, measuring 2 by 4 inches. After learning the history of the *financier*, of course J. *et* G. tried this little loaf again in the stock market pâtisserie. (See page 116.)

The *pain aux raisins* has not yet been satisfactorily described in American terms, so here is more detail.

Pain aux Raisins

To begin with, raisin rolls start with a brioche dough: a butter-egg-yeast dough that gives it that unique yeast smell, golden color, full texture, and butter richness not to be found in American coffee rolls. Paris is known for its *brioche mousseline* because it has even more butter than the brioche *ordinaire*. (Most Parisian pastry shops also sell a *croissant ordinaire* or *croissant beurre*—meaning more butter in the dough. For the short time you are in Paris, go for the *extraordinaire* and buy the *croissant beurre*!) Next, after the golden dough is rolled into a rectangle, it is covered with a pastry custard-cream and topped with rum-soaked raisins so that when it is rolled, cut, and baked, there is a thin layer of custard throughout the roll. Usually a light glaze of sugar and water covers the top, but sometimes it is glazed with a little apricot jam (the Parisian favorite in jams), the final touch.

Please notice, there is never a hint of cinnamon in a *pain aux raisins*. In the coffee cakes that we Americans are used to, baked with a heavy hand of cinnamon and brown sugar, one would never notice the subtle butter and custard tastes that make this roll Parisian. No wonder it is out of this world! The golden brioche dough, which is slathered with a light custard-cream, creates a sweet, soft, rich, unforgettable melting experience in your mouth. Savor it! Never wash it down with coffee—hold the coffee until the pastry is safely in your stomach after you have given full justice to this sublime treat.

Jeanette and Georgette sat on the steps of the church in the morning sun, eating their pastries, and then followed a path around the corner to a very small garden outside a small house where the pastor lives. No one was around to answer their queries. It looked like a rural Vermont village, with a small kitchen garden staked out.

When you arrive, you'll never know you are in the middle of the grandest city in the world.

If you get there at lunch time, you'll want to have more than a coffee at the Tabac de la Poste. It was one of the most inviting cafés J. *et* G. had seen. You can get a sandwich (ham or cheese or tomato on a baguette); remember no fats—mayo or butter—on the French sandwiches, so you can later enjoy that pastry cream! Or the *plat du jour* (day's special), or a salad and omelet or a *croque monsieur* (grilled ham and cheese sandwich—always Jeanette's very first taste in Paris, with a glass of red wine). It was "neighborhood only" for diners at this café.

One time when Georgette was double-checking the pastry shops for *Paris by Pastry*, she looked in the window of Rendez-vous Chocolat, 78, rue du Rendez-vous, thinking of her chocolate-loving friend Helen, back in New York City. She went in to bring home a little token of Parisian chocolate and stayed an hour, learning a lot more about chocolate than she'd ever read or heard before from the new owner of the shop. *Très gentille*, she is a French woman who had gone from corporate finance to cosmetics to her own *chocolaterie*. You'll love going into her shop (*haute chocolaterie*), where each bar of chocolate is marked (75% to 90% cocoa) to indicate the percent of chocolate in it! Not only that, but also marked from which country it came —the origin of the cocoa beans. Many are from Africa, Ghana, and Madagascar, for example; also from the Caribbean Islands, Colombia, Ecuador, Peru, as well as Papua New Guinea. Oh yes, madame is the third generation *chocolatière* in her family. Georgette learned that chocolates should be smooth and shiny, from a copperish color to black, and that unlike American chocolate (whose best chocolates are 65% cocoa to 35% sugar), many French customers would not consider eating a chocolate with less than 85% cocoa. Furthermore, Georgette was graciously told that chocolates must always be served at room temperature (65°F), consumed within the month after purchase, and stored in an airtight container in a cool place (55°F). Just think of all the things that Georgette's friend Helen learned along with her token taste of 85% chocolate!

Visiting the third master pastry chef shop took Jeanette and Georgette back to the rich hunting grounds of the 7th arrondissement.

Jean Millet

103, rue St-Dominique, Paris 07
Telephone: 01.45.51.49.80
Metro: La Tour-Maubourg
Closed: Sundays pm, Mondays;
August

A *salon de thé, chocolaterie*, and pâtisserie all in one, Jean Millet used to be run by one of the original five Parisian members of the Association of International Master Pastry Chefs, so you know that nothing even dares to be below an "8+." Exquisite-looking.

Georgette spotted a *croquembouche*, a 2-foot-high pyramid of caramelized puff balls decorated with sugar roses and rose leaves. It has a *nougatine* base (flaked almonds, sugar and butter); the puff pastry balls are filled with pastry cream and whipped cream, usually flavored with Kirsch. Jeanette learned that the *croquembouche* is the traditional pastry for christenings, First Communions, and weddings in France. When it is used for a wedding, often the top is decorated with a marzipan bride and groom. A christening or First Communion calls for flowers or some *dragées* (sugar-coated almonds) decorating the pyramid.

Even after the spectacular, the apricot tart looked *formi* (terrific) to J. *et* G. They had heard that the shop is known for its *financiers*, honey *madeleines,* and *brioches*

mousselines. The brioche is loaded with butter and comes out golden delicious, crispy on the outside and light and custardy in the middle. The *éclairs* are covered with a flat rather than a glossy icing; the *divorcée*, which was €2.50, looked fabulous; the strawberry tart at €4 was shaped like a little boat. *Les petits moelleux au chocolat* were soft chocolate cakes in a cylinder shape with powdered sugar on top for €1.50, and they looked like the best buy. A meringue chocolate *chantilly* for €3 and a *charlotte aux poires* made with ladyfingers and pears folded into pastry cream with red berries decorating the top, were delectable-looking. Jeanette and Georgette knew they had plenty of time to savor the flavor, because they had already selected a bench for their pastry tasting—in the Parc des Invalides, with a view of the Tour Eiffel and the Pont Alexandre III from that very bench. They agreed on the *gâteau aux poires*, a pear cake topped with pastry cream and caramelized sugar, for €2.50. Hearty and very delicious, it was assigned an "8+." *Quelle vue, quelle journée . . . quelle pâtisserie!*

Paris Prizes
According to Jeanette *et* Georgette

When you hang out in Paris for several visits, or spend a semester abroad, or are on a trip with a special interest (stalking the flea markets, the stock market, or the cemeteries), you will go beyond the expectations of a first-time visitor in Paris. Even though Georgette isn't interested in taking a boat down the Seine and spending all of that money getting sea sick, or in shopping at the Galeries Lafayette, Jeanette reminded her that many of their dear readers would love to have dinner at twilight on the Seine and spend their money at the upscale, very magnificent art-nouveau building which was built for Parisian shopping. Pâtisseries that you can visit while studying at the Alliance Française, reading at the Bibliothèque Nationale, as well as hunting to find the Canal St-Martin are all included as "Paris Prizes: According to Jeanette *et* Georgette." With your own special interests in mind, see if you agree. *D'accord?*

Musée Marmottan

2, rue Louis Boilly, Paris 16
Telephone: 01.42.24.07.02
Metro: Muette
Closed: Mondays

Before you get off the metro to visit this delightful upper-middle class *quartier* of Paris, be sure you notice the priorities the French have for seating in the metro. In every car, there are reserved seats for those with special conditions, in the following order of precedence:

1. War wounded
2. Disabled
3. Pregnant women, and children under four years old accompanying an adult
4. Seventy-five years old and older

It's interesting to see a culture's priorities so very clearly spelled out!

Jeanette and Georgette have been going to the Musée Marmottan for years. Even in July and August, it's almost empty. They love the walk from the metro to this museum, which is housed in a grand 19th-century mansion in the 16th arrondissement. (You're in the 16th; enjoy this most chic *quartier* of all of Paris!) There isn't a more beautiful walk to a museum in the world. If you don't have time to take in all of the museums in Paris, just walk to this one, turn around and go back!

You'll be glad you did. There are old trees bordering the sidewalk on each side, deep-green grass even in March, and the buds are all ahead of season on this extraordinary walk. Georgette has never gone to the *musée* without going to the tea salon closest to the metro, often for lunch but at least for a coffee. (Georgette always has time for the tea salon and walk.) Quiet, with a circle of tables holding small lamps with elegant shades, it overlooks the street. This is Paris at its neighborhood best.

There are signs that point the direction to the Marmottan, and they are easy to follow. The thrill of the Marmottan is the more than one hundred paintings, pastels, and drawings by Claude Monet. Among them is a circular gallery exhibiting sixteen of his water-lily paintings. You can stand in the middle and imagine that you are at the edge of Monet's very pond at Giverny. There are also the *Impression: Sunrise,* and *La Barque,* a lavender rowboat in the upper right hand corner of the canvas under an overhang of leaves. And a wonderful train canvas, as well as a snow scene.

On the way back, Georgette became intrigued with

Yamazaki!
6, Chaussée de la Muette, Paris 16,
and Tokyo
Telephone: 01.40.50.19.19

Metro: Muette
Closed: Jamais (Never!)

Ten years ago, J. *et* G. couldn't believe this shop's Japanese name with the most exquisite pastries in the shop window. Going in, Jeanette saw a *pomme au beurre* and a *mousse aux framboises* that looked the best among the many cakes and tarts. Georgette had to ask, "How did this shop get this name??" The clerk replied that it was bought by the Japanese five years ago; they own several pastry shops in Paris, just as they own golf courses in America. But it is run, and all pastries are baked, by French chefs! "Oh," replied Georgette. In the meantime, Jeanette chose a *gâteau aux myrtilles*, a cake wedge in a pastry lining just loaded with little wild blueberries, that translated to "bilberries," or huckleberries, whatever those are. They looked and tasted like first cousins to blueberries to J. *et* G.

Now to find that Parc de Passy, where we could eat our pastry. A neighborhood park in the 16th arrondissement would be perfect for our treat. Walking down about seven blocks . . . Ooops, we must have missed it. Back to the sign and try again. That's funny—it doesn't seem to be here. Let's see, let's go on the other side . . . hmmmm . . . "Jeanette, ask someone!" In one shop, then in

another, after thirty minutes of trying to follow signs and directions, J. *et* G. want to say to you, dear readers: Do not follow signs to Parc de Passy! The relentless J. *et* G. found a bench and devoured their pastry, which was not too sweet and just loaded with those little blue berries. A tiny leaf of mint on top, it got a "9+."

Directly across the street from the Japanese shop they spotted

A la Flûte Enchantée
7, avenue Mozart, Paris 16
Telephone: 01.45.27.05.92
Metro: Muette
Closed: Sundays; no annual vacation

Traditional, the very best, nothing below an "8" in this 16th-arrondissement shop. There were *palets chocolats*, which were shortbread-dough biscuits covered with chocolate, and delectable-looking *pralinettes*, tarts filled with praline cream-custard, topped with powdered sugar and almonds. Jeanette and Georgette were in total agreement that they had never seen a better-looking *pain aux raisins;* it looked as if it were almost all custard, with just a little circle of dough holding it together. Jeanette pointed out to Georgette that this was the third time they had rated a *pain aux raisins* as "the best."

Two doors away, what appeared to be an expensive jewelry shop was instead a *chocolaterie,* the most chic chocolate shop that J. *et* G. could ever imagine. They had never been interested in going into a *chocolaterie,* as there are no pastries, only chocolates, but who could resist this one?

Côté de France Chocolatier

3, avenue Mozart, Paris 16
Telephone: 01.42.88.17.79
Metro: Muette
Closed: Sundays, Mondays

Jeanette and Georgette learned that there are five Côté de France shops in Paris and one in Tokyo. With awards framed and hung about this small shop, and showcases of individual chocolates (none were pre-boxed or wrapped), Georgette expected to see security guards posed by the doors and showcases! The finest of cocoa is used (with no preservatives, *bien sûr que non—* of course not), and the top Gold for chocolates was won by this shop in 1992. Keep in mind, dear reader, that J. *et* G. had just polished off their blueberry wedge and so were not tempted to buy even one of these fine chocolates. But the experience of the shop was worth the time looking at the best in Parisian chocolate shops. It should also be pointed out that although they admit to being pastry freaks, you must have guessed, J. *et* G. are not chocolate nuts.

Musée Rodin

77, rue de Varenne, Paris 07
Telephone: 01.47.05.01.34
Metro: Varenne
Closed: Mondays

It was so hot in July that Jeanette and Georgette decided to pay only for the Rodin garden entrance and to skip the interior of the museum that day. What Georgette had forgotten, and realized in the snack area of the Rodin garden, is how many American families bring their teenagers (who become sullen as soon as they are alone with their parents) to Paris in the summertime, and they all sit and argue in the nicest of places. The only other place with more teenagers and families is at the Café de la Paix at the Place de l'Opéra. But in this lovely sculpture garden, you can take your pastry in hand and walk out amongst the hundreds of rosebushes, sit on the benches, and look at the renowned *Le Penseur* ("The Thinker"), *The Burghers of Calais, The Gates of Hell,* and a statue of Balzac. Everyone knows Rodin, the most famous of French 19th-century sculptors, but not everyone knows that there are also several works here by Camille Claudel, his young model and lover, who became a very talented sculptor. Georgette wants to remind her readers, however, that she is not here to teach art, but to bring a pastry to the art . . .

With this thought in mind, the best and closest pâtisserie is Rollet Pradier (described on page 32) at 32, rue de Bourgogne, Paris 07, which you will find right across from the National Assembly. It is a very chic and elegant pâtisserie, *traiteur,* and *chocolaterie.* To our chocoholic readers, Jeanette and Georgette stress that the pastry chefs go heavy on the chocolate. The *religieuse* was covered all over with thick, deep, dark chocolate. You can get lunch or *un petit goûter* (a little snack), or simply buy a pastry to take to the Rodin garden and nibble outside amid the roses and sculpture.

Palais de Tokyo

J. et G. began the day searching for the newly (2006) remodeled Musée d'Art Moderne de la Ville de Paris, the 20th-century art collection of the city of Paris in the Palais de Tokyo (13, avenue du Président Wilson), in the 16th arrondissement quite near the Palais de Chaillot at Trocadéro. Georgette always thinks she is at Trocadéro when she is really at the Palace of Tokyo. The curved wings of the Palace of Tokyo look like the Palace of Chaillot to her. They are one bridge apart from each other, and both have a spectacular view of the Tour Eiffel. You can easily spend a day in the three adjoining buildings which are filled with exhibits of architecture, French maritime history, French cinema, modern art shows, and works by Matisse and Dufy. Modern and expansive are the feelings that will take over, causing stalkers of the sweet life to search for their pastries before they get there. Getting off the metro at Alma Marceau, J. et G. decided to walk straight up avenue George V toward the Champs-Elysées to see the American Cathedral on their way to find the best pastries of the chic 16th arrondissement.

The American Cathedral on 23, avenue George V, also known as the Church of the Holy Trinity, Church of England, didn't distract the pastry-hunters for long because they decided to look it all over some other time when they could return for a service, rather than a tourist-look when they were so hungry for their pastries. Leaving the cathedral, they were wondering how on earth anyone manages to find the pastry shops of the 16th when they spotted an oldish Parisian woman with shopping bag in hand going straight up the hill on avenue George V. They decided to follow her. Hurrying after her, Georgette stopped the Parisian with, *"Pardonnez-moi Madame, mais où allez-vous pour acheter vos pâtisseries?"* Whereupon she responded, *"Rue de Chaillot, suivez-moi!"* (Follow me!) So, they followed her down rue Quentin, crossing avenue Marceau, and *voilà!* A small street of exquisite *boulangeries* (bakeries—mainly bread), pâtisseries, *charcuteries* (delis), *fromageries* (cheese shops), and *beaucoup de boutiques à la mode.* They knew their pastry guide knew where she was going!

Now of course our dear readers don't have to take such an indirect route—they can go directly to rue de Chaillot. Hard to believe, but you can begin your pastry hunt very near the Modern Museum of Art, in the most exclusive, most traditionally chic arrondissement of Paris, the famous 16th, by simply walking from the metro on avenue du Président Wilson toward the

museum until you come to rue Freycinet. Go up the hill until you reach rue de Chaillot on your right. Jeanette reminded Georgette that life can be so simple if only you know where you are going!

Mi Do Ré Chaillot
41, rue de Chaillot, Paris 16
Telephone: 01.47.20.85.10
Metro: Iéna, Alma Marceau
Closed: Sundays, Mondays;
August

To tell you the truth, Jeanette and Georgette had to return to this pâtisserie because they got into an argument about the name. Jeanette was sure that it was "Do Ré Mi." Georgette was sure it wasn't because she had gotten a kick out of its *not* being "Do Ré Mi" when she first saw it. Readers, you know who paid for the next pastry! Although the name of the shop is amusing, the pastries looked so-so and weren't up to their usual standards. Looking across the street, the stalkers spotted

Malitourne
30, rue de Chaillot, Paris 16
Telephone: 01.47.20.52.26
Metro: Iéna, Alma Marceau
Closed: Sundays pm, Mondays;
August

This exquisite pastry shop was more like it—with its marble floor and sparkling glass showcases.

Bavaroise Enrubanée au Chocolat et Grand Marnier

If for this reason alone, J. *et* G. will purposely go back to Paris just to taste again this scrumptious pastry. It is lined with a thin layer of striped chocolate-and-vanilla sponge cake, brushed with Grand Marnier, then filled with a chocolate cream and marbleized with a Grand Marnier cream. Finally, this one was topped with chocolate curls. The angels must dine in Paris . . .

Malitourne lived up to J.'s *et* G.'s high expectation of nothing below a "9," exactly what a 16th-arrondissement pastry shop should look, smell, and taste like. Of course, the well-exercised stalkers knew that a fruit tart is always a superb pastry, but no, this time they considered a pastry that they not only had never tried, but also had never heard of: a puff-pastry tart with banana cream, covered with chocolate rum sauce! *Ooooh, là là!* But wait! The hunters realized that they were on their way to the museum and that chocolate rum sauce should be eaten while sitting down. *Donc*

(so), Jeanette said that she could have another *puits d'amour,* and Georgette considered the *trocadéro,* but instead they chose a tart with cream and a caramelized top—do you know it? A *paris-brest* that earned a "9" without their so much as looking at one another. Well, what it took was only one look, one bite, one swallow, one word: "Nine!" They had taken so long to find the best pastry shop near the Modern Art Museum that they ate it on the spot.

Continuing on rue de Chaillot until they came to avenue Marceau, the pastry pals walked down the hill toward the Modern Art

Museum, where they spotted another pastry shop that looked almost like a department store, with a hostess greeting the shoppers as they entered the automatic glass door.

Traiteur Noura

29, avenue Marceau, Paris 16
Telephone: 01.47.23.02.20
Metro: Alma Marceau
Open: Every day until midnight

Something about this shop didn't seem familiar to the two pastry-hunters—the window had many dried fruits, and pastries with figs and dates, reminding them of the Jewish pâtisseries in the *quartier* Marais—until they realized it was a combination Lebanese-French pastry shop. It looked like "a jewel"—perfection. They gazed first at a *bavaroise,* then at a *tarte chaillot,* some tiny little *mille-feuilles* (napoleons), and a *paris-brest* (a pastry puff with coffee cream in the middle, topped with almonds and powdered sugar) for €2; a *mousse au citron* (lemon mousse) for €2.20; and some Lebanese pastries such as *maamoul* (a small cake with pistachios and dates) for €1.20 and an *aiche al sarail* (a cream with almonds and dried fruits) for €4. Jeanette got to choose the *bavaroise enrubannée au chocolat et Grand Marnier* while Georgette was busy writing in her notebook.

Dear readers, have you forgotten where we are going? Why, to the museum, *bien sûr!* You remember— just keep walking down avenue Marceau until you come to avenue du Président Wilson. Take a right, and a very short walk will bring you to the

Musée d'Art Moderne de la Ville de Paris

11, avenue du Président Wilson, Paris 16
Telephone: 01.53.67.40.00
Metro: Alma Marceau
Closed: Mondays

You will first of all see the remarkable sculptures by Gabriel Forestier on the doorway. This museum is known for its special exhibitions of 20th-century art, and the first Pierre Bonnard retrospective in twenty-two years reopened the remodeled museum. But don't miss the biggest painting in the world from the permanent collection, Raoul Dufy's *Spirit of Electricity,* a huge mural created for the 1937 World's Fair depicting scientists who mastered the form of energy. Also in the Tokyo Palace are two theatres of the Cinémathèque Française—Oh, no! There used to be two theatres— they have just (2006) moved to a new museum at 51, rue de Bercy, in the 12th arrondissement. (A third one is at Trocadéro, in the Palace of Chaillot). At the Tokyo Palace you can see famous film archives and repertory theatre at film screenings in the French film and television school FEMIS. Anyone can see the classical films of Jean-Luc Godard and François Truffaut on Tuesday through Sunday evenings from 6:30 to 9 PM for €6.

Bibliothèque Nationale

58, rue de Richelieu, Paris 01
Telephone: 01.47.03.81.26
Metro: Bourse
Closed: Sundays

Georgette knows that there is a new national library in Paris, the Bibliothèque de France, and she knows, too, that the 19th-century reading room of the old Bibliothèque Nationale is open only to scholars. Not one to take *"non"* for an answer, she persuaded Jeanette to carry her notebook in one hand, a pencil in the other, look "all business," and just walk right through the security post with her. The young woman who guarded the gate to a simply spectacular room of cast-iron columns and vaulted curves of iron latticework, long study tables, and hushed silence, simply asked, *"Est-ce que vous êtes étudiantes?"* *"Oui, bien sûr!"* and they walked right in! Georgette was so excited to be there, she hardly knew what to do next. But thinking back at the hours she had spent working in the public reading room in the Boston Public Library, she quickly looked for two seats among the study tables, put her things down, got Jeanette (who was afraid they would be put in jail any minute) to sit down, and they just spent the afternoon in scholarly research, silence, and meditation.

Pastry research always uppermost in their minds, it was hard for the researchers to believe that this historic building from the 17th century with more than nine million books, including two Gutenberg Bibles, manuscripts of Proust and Hugo, and first editions of Rabelais, could also house vending machines with overpriced Cokes, Oranginas, Kit Kats, M&Ms, and that all-American favorite, Snickers bars. Well, J. *et* G. will admit to having had a Coke. However, when you walk out the front door into the charming little Square Rameau with a fountain in the center and shade trees all around, your pastry-trained eyes will find

Gérant Rodrigues Gérard

6, rue Rameau, Paris 02
Telephone: 01.42.96.81.91
Metro: Bourse
Closed: Saturdays, Sundays; first week of August

After the thrill of seeing the majestic reading room of the National Library, Jeanette and

Georgette were in the mood for a princely pastry. With nothing in the shop below a "7" in appearance, they chose a classic French

Délice aux Cassis

Mais qu'est-ce que c'est? (Just what is it?) A mixture of black-currant syrup and purée is soaked into the sponge base of a ring flan. Then Italian meringue is folded into a black-currant custard made of gelatin leaves, milk, vanilla, egg yolks, black-currant purée, and sugar. When the custard is well blended, whipped cream is mixed in, and the custard is immediately poured over the sponge base to fill the flan ring until level. After it is chilled, the mousse is glazed with black-currant purée, and it is topped with whole black currants rolled in sugar.

Sitting on a bench in the shade in Square Rameau, J. *et* G. mused over their wonderful afternoon's educational fulfillment that took place in the beauty of the Bibliothèque Nationale—and its rewarding aftermath, the sensual pleasure of taste and texture of a *délice aux cassis*. Ah, only in Paris.

Canal St-Martin

It took Jeanette and Georgette ten summers of Paris living before they even heard about the Canal of St-Martin. Jeanette said that even though Georgette couldn't think of anything worse than taking a two-and-a-half-hour boat trip through the canals and the Seine of northern Paris, that it should be mentioned just in case some of their dear readers had different interests than Georgette. Reluctantly, Georgette agreed to include the Website—www.canauxrama.com—that tells the whole canal barge story. "They say" you can see the old landmarks of the Edith Piaf, blue-collar factory workers of the 19th century in this neighborhood. Take the iron footbridges to cross the canal; you can watch the fishermen, the river barges, and locks.

Georgette says it's just not worth it! Jeanette says she would have to be back in Paris another ten years before she'd bother again with the canals. However, if their dear readers had rather go by "they say," than "Jeanette and Georgette sez," then at the first footbridge look for

La Bonne Fournée
Boulangerie-Pâtisserie
J.P. Thouseau
151, Quai de Valmy, Paris 10
Telephone: 01.42. 05. 43. 83
Metro: Louis Blanc
Closed: Sundays, Mondays; August

This shop had a whole baked apple on a tart for €1.50, and a rhubarb tart, but nothing looked good enough to buy. Georgette admits it was hot. There was a July heat wave, and even the tree-lined quays didn't cool her off. But J. *et* G. felt even hotter when they realized they had spent a whole day looking for pastry shops and never even found one that had anything above a "3"! No one goes to Paris to seek the ethnic streets with Korean, Italian, Chinese, and Arab pastry shops, but if Georgette was wrong . . . go to Canal St-Martin, start at metro Louis Blanc, walk on the iron footbridges, see the Barrière de la Villette, (a toll house from the 1700s), but . . . take your French baguette and pastry with you to enjoy those benches beneath the shade of the trees along the canal. Or keep walking toward the Place de la République and go to

Daniel Duc Nhon
G. Leroux
27, rue du Faubourg du Temple, Paris 10
Telephone: 01.48.03.06.82
Metro: République
Closed: Weekends; August

There was a very slim choice of pastries, but what they had looked excellent and the *pain aux raisins* looked unusually good. Jeanette and Georgette selected the rhubarb tart and took it to a bench near a carrousel. Looking up at the statue of the allegory to the République de France reminded Georgette of Marianne. (You remember, dear readers, don't you, that Marianne is the "Uncle Sam" of France?) They ate their tasty *tarte à la rhubarbe,* giving it a "9" even after their hot and disappointing walk. What is hot? It was even too hot for children to ride on the carrousel—the musical carrousel went round and round and round, with nary a child in sight.

Marché aux Puces de St-Ouen (Flea Market)

Even first-year high school French students learn about this famous Paris flea market. And Jeanette and Georgette know very well how to get there, because their apartment is located at the same metro stop, Porte de Clignancourt.

Therefore, you can be sure they know best where to get a pastry, and perhaps a sandwich before you set off on the 10- to 15-minute walk to the old and new wares amongst the acres and acres of flea market. Get off the metro at Clignancourt, cross the very busy (speeding cars) boulevard Ornano, and very close to the metro stop and main path to the flea market you will find

Gambini Yves

80, boulevard Ornano, Paris 18
Telephone: 01.46.06.00.61
Metro: Porte de Clignancourt
Closed: Wednesdays; no annual vacation

Key here, is that this pâtisserie is open all day Sunday, because Saturday and Sunday are the days of the flea market. It's a small, typical French neighborhood pastry shop in a *quartier* that is fast becoming more Arab- and U.S.-fast-foods honky-tonk than French. Why, it even has a Burger King opposite this shop. Gambini Yves is the only place to go.

They have exceptionally good sandwiches (*baguettes* of ham and cheese, or tomato and lettuce), for €2 to €4; and yes, traditional fruit tarts, *éclairs, charlottes,* and *mille-feuilles,* as well. Over the years, Jeanette and Georgette have judged the pastries at least a "7" and once up to a "9." But since

the food possibilities in the flea market are very limited, and the metro stop has gone toward fast foods, these sandwiches and pastries seem like (or at least are appreciated as much as) a "10" anywhere else!

With lunch in hand, do go at least once to the market, where you will find furniture, 19th-century decorative arts, china, old jewelry, loads of paintings, records, new and old clothes, silver, umbrellas, African art, and always, some piece of tapestry or lace, or a 200-year-old plate that you can't live without and can easily pack to carry on the plane home. Georgette couldn't live without a pastel painting of roses in a gold frame, and she hand-carried it home on Air France, putting it in back of the last seat in the cabin. Jeanette had to have a very beautiful blue-and-bright-yellow plate from the 19th century, which she hand-carried to her Connecticut home. There is big business at the flea market and many of the stalls even take credit cards.

You will meet the challenge of a day at the flea market much more easily if you make sure that you have your lunch and a bottle of water in hand . . . before you go! Or if you want to go to a restaurant in the flea market, as Jeanette, Georgette, *et* brother John did one time, you are in for very

touristy, good-natured fun at Chez Louisette! It is open from 8 AM until 6 PM on Saturdays, Sundays, and Mondays. You don't go there for the food, but go for the fun of it. Everyone loves to be there listening to the Edith Piaf music in the background. When you need to sit for a while after hunting the fleas' treasures, make your way to 130, avenue Michelet for the only hot spot at the flea market!

Palais de la Bourse

CEOs traveling to Paris for business may want to start their visit with a *financier* at the Palais de la Bourse (stock exchange) rather than with a *religieuse* at Notre-Dame! In 1808, Napoleon commissioned the construction of the present building, with its sixty-four Corinthian columns, which was finished in 1826. You may go inside and watch the traders in action from the spectators' gallery. There is a guided tour every 30 minutes from 11 AM to 1 PM, Monday through Friday, and two tours daily at noon and 12:30 from July 1 to September 15. Call the Bourse for more information at 01.42.89.70.00.

But don't get started on an empty stomach, as Jeanette and Georgette did, because they couldn't find a decent pastry in sight of three blocks in any direction from the Palais de la Bourse! If you've arrived at the Bourse just in time for a tour, and don't have time for a *financier* and the charming fountain sight, then settle for Riva Sandwiches, 1, rue du Quatre Septembre, or Bread and Best Self-Gritt on rue St-Marc, which are the best bets compared to the many other cafeterias in the area. The next time they go, J. *et* G. will pick up their sandwich *à emporter* (to go) at the Boulangerie de la Fountaine Gaillon and skip the easy-to-come by, ordinary choices closest to the Bourse. Profit from their experience and go first to the

Boulangerie de la Fountaine Gaillon

15, rue Gaillon, Paris, 02
Telephone: 01.47.42.22.49
Metro: Bourse
Closed: Sundays, Mondays

At the Bourse metro stop, find rue Filles St-Thomas, which turns into rue St-Augustin, which runs into Place Gaillon. Or, if you aren't in the mood for a four-block walk before your breakfast pastry, get off at metro Opéra and walk down the avenue de l'Opéra until you come to rue Gaillon on your left.

Here, you will find the most wonderful breakfast breads in the whole Bourse area. Don't expect a friendly place—J. *et* G. have been there several times, and no matter who is working, friendly is not a concept that comes to mind. But nothing below an "8" is in this wonderful shop where you will want to sit at the counter looking out at the fountain, rather than in at the scowling help.

There are eight stools lined up at a copper counter facing the window and looking out on a very small, delightful square with a lovely fountain built into the back wall of a hotel. The fountain spouts from a lion's mouth as a cherub pierces a fish.

You can choose the best *pain aux raisins* that Jeanette and Georgette have ever had in Paris (so far!). Or a *baba au rhum,* which they had on their second trip to this shop, which was much later in the day. The *baba* has great balance in the rum-soaked yeast pastry—not too strong and not too sweet, but perfectly satisfying, singing out for an espresso to follow while you look out at the sparkling fountain. Or choose the *brioche au chocolat,* one or two of a variety of croissants, some *beignets aux pommes* (apple-filled doughnuts), or best of all, choose a *financier* while you are at the Bourse! The *financier* is an almond cake that looks like a little gold brick, and along with the *madeleine,* is the most popular morning snack in Paris among the French. While we were rating the crusty outside and the warm, moist almond flavor inside, Jeanette announced that she wasn't going home without this recipe, as she wanted to make them for her French class so that her students would learn that all French pastries are not chocolate. Georgette reminded Jeanette that she couldn't make them at home without the special molds, and if they got the recipe, they had to tell their readers where to buy the *financier* tin molds as well. They agreed that Jeanette would get the recipe and Georgette would find a kitchenware shop that sells the financier mold. *Voilà!* the recipe:

Financier

    1 cup almonds
    1^2/$_3$ cups powdered sugar
    ^{1}/$_2$ cup all-purpose flour
    6 egg whites
    ^{3}/$_4$ cup sweet butter, melted and cooled

    18 *financier* molds (each measures 2x4 inches)

Preheat the over to 450°F degrees. Toast the almonds on a baking sheet until browned, about 5 minutes. Grind the cooled almonds to a fine powder in a food processor. In a bowl, combine the sugar, ground almonds, and flour, and sift the mixture through a fine sieve into another bowl. Jeanette was told by the chef that this mixture must be very fine. Stir in the unbeaten egg whites until blended, then stir in the butter until well blended. Butter the molds and fill each mold almost to the top. Place the tins on a thick baking sheet for a crusty cake and place in the oven. Bake for 7 minutes, then reduce heat to 400°F degrees and bake another 7 minutes. Turn off the heat and let the *financiers* rest in the oven another 7 minutes. Remove the *financiers* from the oven and place upside down on a wire rack until they come out of the mold.

Georgette did her homework and learned that our readers can find the *financier* molds (and *madeleine* and *cannelés* molds as well, *bien sûr*) at the very upscale, chic Culinarion, 99, rue de Rennes, Paris 06. Take the metro to Rennes, where you can buy them directly, or visit the Web site (www.culinarion.com) to purchase them or request a catalog. You can also find pastry molds in the housewares department section at the department store La Samaritaine near Pont Neuf, where Georgette always buys wallpaper to take home for her Vermont house. But *hélas,* we have learned the store is now closed for restoration and it could be years before it is back in business—*zut alors!* (Darn!)

Jeanette wants Georgette to tell our dear readers about another real shopping treat. (Jeanette would do anything to get Georgette to shop, which she detests, unless it involves food, housewares, glasses frames, or shoes.) Here it is—the hardware store of hardware stores of the world, the BHV (Le Bazaar de l'Hôtel de Ville). It has tools, paint, cookware, camping gear, every size and shape nail, hook, screw, lock—you name it. And on the third floor you will realize that if you can't find a pastry mold or any piece of cooking equipment that you can think of—you won't want it! BHV is at 52-64 rue de Rivoli, Paris 04, telephone:

01.42.74.90.00. There is even a special metro entrance (Hôtel de Ville) to the hardware section which is the BHV basement, and not only that, but a little café where Georgette has sat down with a *café et tarte tatin.* All in a retro design of old hardware. When Georgette needed a plug for a bathtub in a rented apartment, brother John led her to BHV for her first visit. Her last visit there was to buy a blow-up mattress for the apartment, which was much cheaper than another bedroom! At that time, Georgette learned that there is also an upstairs with clothes and things, but the excitement is all in the hardware, metro level!

If by chance you are an armchair travel reader, and have no intention of going to Paris and its hardware stores, and you don't want to pay the postage from *la belle France,* then get your pastry molds from your local kitchenware store or Williams-Sonoma on the Web (www.Williams-Sonoma.com). Georgette even surfed the Web for her dear readers and learned that if they perform a Google search for "silicone pastry molds," they will find *beaucoup de possibilités.*

Jardin des Plantes

Take the metro to the Gare d'Austerlitz metro stop, where you will find three exits: (1) Grandes Lignes (major railway lines), (2) boulevard de l'Hôpital, and (3) Jardin des Plantes. Go up the escalator leading to the Jardin des Plantes, and there, right at the top of the steps you will find

Boulangerie-Pâtisserie de la Gare
boulevard de l'Hôpital, Paris 12
Telephone: 01.47.07.21.95
Metro: Gare d'Austerlitz
Closed: Saturday pm

It's the only pastry shop anywhere near the Jardin des Plantes. So if you haven't taken one with you, there are large wedges of pastries, but nothing above a "7." We tried our early-morning *pain aux raisins,* and while Georgette gave it a "3," Jeanette wouldn't rise above a "2"! Georgette's brother John from the Netherlands was with them and she was trying to impress him with her knowledge of where to go for the best . . . so they all hurried right over to rue Delambre in the 14th arrondissement to prove her point.

But not before a tour of the area. Botanists and families who want to take their children to the Natural History Museum will love the Jardin des Plantes much more than will gardeners or lovers looking for beautiful flowers. It doesn't have the landscaping of the Brooklyn Botanical Gardens, and there appeared more gravel and

dust than flora.

On your way back to the metro, you won't miss McDonalds on rue Buffon and boulevard de l'Hôpital. There you will find all the comforts of home without leaving half a euro: restrooms, air conditioning in case you, too, hit a heat wave, and, oh yes, hot water for washing those pastried fingers.

Père Lachaise

It's hard to believe that with the hippie cult following Jim Morrison (The Doors) to his resting place in the cemetery, and with the large number of Arab-owned businesses at its entrance, that one could expect to find a decent pastry shop near Père Lachaise . . . but here it is:

Pâtisserie Guy et Colombe Maquin
7, Place Auguste Métivier,
Paris 20
Metro: Père Lachaise
Closed: Sundays; August

A pear tartlet looked superb; a *tarte aux framboises* in a basket was artistically presented, as were a mocha vanilla cake, and several cakes with almonds and with nosegays of *petites violettes* on top, further embellished with exquisite little green leaves. The pear tartlet was a vanilla upside-down cake on a shortbread pastry with half a pear on the top, glazed with a gelatin topping. This very thin glaze gave the tart a moist and glossy look, and along with the crispy crust, you get four textures in one bite: the pastry, cake, pear, and gelatin glaze! As J. *et* G. sat on a bench in the cemetery, as close as one can get to Edith Piaf's grave, the pastry easily won a "9+."

You may want to carry your own pastry to the gravesite of Marcel Proust, Simone Signoret, Yves Montand, Sarah Bernhardt, or Oscar Wilde, depending on your literary mood. If you plan to take your pastry to The Doors' lead singer, be prepared to run when the *agents de police* chase you away because of the graffiti and the general disturbing of the peace that takes place around Jim Morrison's grave. Jeanette and Georgette had to admit that they were curious since they had visited his grave twice in the mid-1970s to get photos for Georgette's daughter and Jeanette's high school classroom *(bien sûr!)*. No longer is a bandanna tied around the head and a joint stuck in the mouth of Jim Morrison's bust; the monument has long since been stolen.

Cité Universitaire
19, boulevard Jourdan, Paris 14
Telephone: 01.45.89.68.52
Metro: RER B from St-Michel to Cité

Georgette wanted to ride on the RER out to the Cité Universitaire, the first place she ever stayed in Paris, back when she was a university student. (It's the same RER that goes to Orly Airport, but if you haven't yet been on an RER, take this one. It's fun!) To this day, if you want inexpensive housing in Paris, there are two places to check first: the bulletin board at the American Church, on the Seine in the 7th arrondissement (tel. 01.47.05.17.99), which has a listing of rooms (often bedrooms in the homes of Americans living in Paris), and the Cité Universitaire. This student residence was built in the 1920s for foreign students studying at the University of Paris, but in the summer anyone can stay for short periods of time. The International House was donated by John D. Rockefeller, and has a restaurant, swimming pool and theatre. There are 37 houses with students from all over the world staying there. The Asian and Armenian houses look Asian and Armenian, and they found out that the Swiss and Dutch residences were actually designed by architects from Switzerland and the Netherlands.

If you go to the International House, you will find a cafeteria with cold drinks, coffee, and stand-up counters like the ones you find in airports. The pastries weren't up to Jeanette's and Georgette's standards, so they hiked two and a half blocks (in a heat wave) to a pastry shop at 78, rue Amiral Mouchez, a major street where Paris buses are garaged and where they begin their daily run. There is a wonderful park (closed on Mondays) to which you can take your pastry if you don't stay on the grounds of the Cité Universitaire, which is also a good place for your treat. Parc Montsouris is a very big park, right across the street from the Cité. You can go to the university via metro and return to the center of Paris by bus #21, which that will take you to la Place de l'Opéra, to the Louvre, the Palais de Justice, or even to the Luxembourg Gardens. And, of course, the bus will give you the beautiful sights of Paris all the way.

Galeries Lafayette

40, boulevard Haussmann,
Paris 09
Telephone: 01.42.82.34.56
Metro: Chaussée-d'Antin, Opéra
Closed: Sundays

Opened in 1906, this beautiful department store is arranged in floors of galleries beneath a magnificent dome of colored glass and wrought iron. An art-nouveau staircase leads to all *étages* (floors). The vista of Paris from the roof is overwhelming.

Starting with the Galeries Lafayette Gourmet, Jeanette and Georgette found that the cafeteria features some very passable pastries such as the traditional puffs and tarts, plus cheesecake and forest cake, mostly for #2. There is a coffee bar with high round tables and stools, so that J. *et* G. took their coffee *éclair* (there were no *divorcées* so that each could have her own flavor) into the coffee bar to see what others were doing. Everyone else was having only coffee, but several people looked at them enviously. Imagine! Sharing a sweet, followed by coffee, all in the same place! Ingenuity comes with experience, *n'est-ce pas?*

They walked up the stairs to the roof, where they agreed: an incomparable vista of the Right Bank's rooftops can be seen all the way to the Sacré-Coeur, which is true north in Paris. J. *et* G. had so often looked at Paris from the Sacré-Coeur while up on Montmartre, but they had never been high enough before to look back. Many paintings and photographs of the Parisian rooftops must have been inspired from this tenth-floor rooftop of the Galeries Lafayette.

Bateaux-mouches

If you plan to take a *bateau-mouche* (pleasure boat) cruise on the Seine, you may board at Pont de l'Alma. The closest good pastry shop is right across the bridge on the Left

Bank on avenue Rapp. Be sure to take the pastry you like best with you—remember, there are no "8s," "9s," or "10s" other than in the pastry shops, the only exception being in four-star restaurants.

**Boulangerie
Félice Lapelusa**
*16, avenue Rapp, Paris 07
Telephone: 01.45.51.66.39
Metro: Pont de l'Alma
Closed: Sundays*

With no boat departure before 10 AM, you will have plenty of time to find your way to this "boulangerie," more like a snack store than a French pastry shop. You will find cold drinks, candy bars, chips, pasta salads, and sandwiches. Long line, and friendly—it must be good! When you stand in the middle of the bridge (Pont de l'Alma) on your way back to the *bateaux-mouches*, you will see the spires of the American churches, the Louvre between the golden angels on Pont Alexander III right in front of you, the Eiffel Tower in back of you, and the Seine alive with boats below you. Oh, Paris . . . how lucky to be here!

Alliance Française
*101, boulevard Raspail, Paris 06
Telephone: 01.45.44.38.28
Metro: St-Placide, Notre-Dame-des-Champs*

Parlez-vous français? Non? Désirez-vous parler français? Oui? Bon! Allez à l'Alliance Française!

Georgette has probably had more French lessons at the Alliance Française than just about any student who has ever walked the halls of this language school. She even has a certificate of attendance for one month in August. Besides learning the four best pastry shops in the *quartier*, Georgette was always thrilled with just being there. In class. With students from all over the world. One time when she took a two-hour morning class, she was the only student from an English-speaking country! No British, Australians, New Zealanders, Canadians, none! Do you understand what that means? If the student doesn't know the word, the teacher gives another word *en français*, not in English, as we do in American classrooms. French is the common language. Yikes . . . it's exciting! And not expensive. And then there are intensive classes, lasting four hours a day. Anyone can go to register on the first of any month of the year, take a test (*oui, en français*—Jeanette refused to take the test for Georgette—a good thing for G.!), and off you go. At one point, Georgette figured that if she were in Paris for three weeks, it would pay to take the month's course. If she were rich, she wouldn't hesitate to take it for even two weeks and pay the month's rate. The Alliance Française in Paris (they have 1,300 schools in 122 countries, so you can go to the Alliance all over the world), is an experience that any francophile has to have.

But first. If you take the metro to St-Placide, you will want to pick up your morning and "going home" pastry right across from the top of the metro as you exit:

Meslay
5, rue Notre-Dame-des-Champs, Paris 06
Telephone: 01.45.48.16.92
Metro: St-Placide, Notre-Dame-des-Champs
Closed: Sundays pm, Mondays; August

As you come up out of the metro at St-Placide, Meslay is a few steps away, right across the street, on the way to the Alliance Française. A pâtisserie with a line for bread, pastries, sandwiches, beverages (Coca Light, Orangina, water), and a few salads; the pastries are "8s" and above. Georgette usually grabbed a *pain aux raisins* on her way to the Alliance, but often Jeanette would meet her after class at the metro stop, at which time they would ponder the *spécialités*. One of the most memorable was the

Petits Coeurs de Fromage Blanc aux Fruits Rouges

(Little cheese cake hearts with red fruits)
This simple dessert is made of *fromage blanc* (equal quantities of cottage cheese and plain yogurt with a taste of lemon juice blended until smooth and creamy) molded into a heart shape and chilled. A double cream is poured over the heart and topped with a few each of strawberries, wild strawberries, raspberries, gooseberries, and red currants. Given the cream sauce, it's best to eat it there . . . but it will carry *(c'est possible, ça)*. After a two- or four-hour French class, you will often want to head for the Jardin du Luxembourg (Luxembourg Gardens) to study, relax and to eat your pastry!

When Jeanette meets Georgette at the Alliance, especially when American friends are visiting them in Paris, and they feel like getting away from the student section and want to hit the designer stuff, they walk toward St-Germain-des-Prés. In that case they walk down boulevard Raspail for two blocks until they come to rue de Rennes, taking a right which goes toward the Seine, and toward boulevard St-Germain-des-Prés, and toward a top pâtisserie. Nothing below a "9 + " can be found at

M. Chevalier
81, rue de Rennes, Paris 06
Metro: Rennes
Telephone: 01.45.48.26.33
Closed: Sundays, Mondays

or at
Ladurée
21, rue Bonaparte, Paris 06
Metro: St-Germain-des-Prés
Telephone: 01.44.07.64.87

Pâtisserie, *oui*. Two elegant places for a sit-down, expensive lunch— *oui, oui!* Jeanette and Georgette chose their pastry to eat later, after their picnic lunch on the bench at Square Laurent Prache, in the shadow of St-Germain-des-Prés Church. You will find it right off rue Bonaparte on rue de l'Abbaye. There's a tiny circle of benches

within sight of the *trop chers* (too expensive) Deux Magots, the renowned Café de Flore, and Paris's oldest church, the 11th-century St-Germain-des-Prés. Unless there is another *Paris by Pastry* pastry-hunter on the bench, you will probably be the only one gazing at Picasso's bust of poet Guillaume Apollinaire (1880-1916). Jeanette wanted to describe the St-Germain-des-Prés area for their readers, to say a word or two about the Deux Magots and the Café de Flore, and surely to talk about the Beaux-Arts section, rue Jacob and rue des Beaux-Arts. Georgette said, *"Non, absolument pas! C'est trop populaire, ça.* Every guide book in the world will tell their dear readers about the *quartier* St-Germain-des-Prés."

The two pastry-hunting pals opened their prize from the pâtisserie on rue de Rennes: a *noyer*, made of an almond-flavored shortbread dough, filled with *crème de marron* (chestnut-flavored pastry cream), and topped with caramelized sugar and walnuts. Georgette magnanimously gave Jeanette the "bigger half." They sat gazing at Apollinaire, enjoying their "10"-rated pastry, and *encore une fois* (once again) gave thanks for the magnificent City of Light.

Que pensez-vous ?
(What do you think?)

You know Jeanette's and Georgette's opinions of Paris *pâtisseries* and their pastries. Now J. *et* G. are eager to hear what you, their readers, think. What is your opinion? Did you find a pastry shop, or taste a pastry that you think deserves to be included in the next edition? Or did you go to a shop or eat a pastry that didn't even begin to live up to your expectations? One that Jeanette gave a "9" and you thought was a "4"? Or the other way around—a *pain aux raisins*, for example, that didn't win more than a "3" from Georgette, but you know that's just unfair! Then, dear readers, *écrivez* (write)! *Dites-leur tout de suite!* Tell them immediately about your delicious discoveries of the sweet life on the streets of Paris!

ParisbyPastry@aol.com

J. *et* G.
Jones Books
309 N. Hillside Terrace
Madison, Wisconsin 53705-3328
U.S.A.

Georgette et Jeanette have lived in Paris, studied in Paris, taken high school groups to Paris, taken their children to Paris, stayed in hotels in Paris, rented apartments in Paris, and have concentrated on pastry shops as a central theme of their Paris visits each year for many years. Known by friends as true francophiles, Georgette (Joyce Slayton Mitchell) is also a college advisor at an independent school in New York City, and the author of 35 nonfiction books, including *Winning the Heart of the College Admissions Dean* (Ten Speed Press, 2001, 2005). Jeanette (Beverly A. Thomas) is known best as a French teacher with a diploma from the Sorbonne and co-taster of Paris pastries. She says that it is only because Paris is such a beautiful walking city that she is able to even consider sharing a pastry every two hours with her hunting pal. *Mesdames* Georgette *et* Jeanette's extensive in-depth knowledge of French culture and literature will enhance every pastry-stalker's delicious Parisian experience.

Photo Credits: All photos by Georgette avec the camera of Jeanette.

Index

Index

PASTRIES, DOUGHS, & FILLINGS

Index

Index